Insights of a Yogi

Understanding Karma through Life's Experiences

Mish Mockovic Martin

BALBOA.
PRESS

A DIVISION OF HAY HOUSE

Images by Mish Mockovic Martin

Balboa Press books may be ordered through booksellers or by contacting:

Balboa Press
A Division of Hay House
1663 Liberty Drive
Bloomington, IN 47403
www.balboapress.com.au
1 (877) 407-4847

Printed in the United States of America.

ISBN: 978-1-4525-2580-8 (sc)
ISBN: 978-1-4525-2579-2 (e)

Balboa Press rev. date: 10/08/2014

For Evie, Sol, and Kenna

CONTENTS

ACKNOWLEDGEMENTS

I wish to thank Lyn and Mark Betar for their constant support; Annie Scully, a true wordsmith; Sarah Ward, a master in grammar and syntax; Scott Leeton, a patient and kind soul; Li Halpin, a true friend; Nigel Rowe, for his knowledge and expertise; Chris Martin, for his encouragement and persistence; and my beautiful yogis, who are a continual source of inspiration and true examples of honesty and dedication.

A NOTE FROM THE AUTHOR

I wanted to write this book to share with you a concept I believe could be the turning point in your life. In fact, this concept is so simple that people never try or even think of trying it. I speak from experience, as I was also such a person. Had I not had the opportunity to undertake this journey, which at times needed more courage and strength than I could muster, I would have never believed it possible. The reward for my physical pain and suffering, emotional distress, and mental fatigue appear insignificant compared to the joy and happiness I feel today. All I know is love, and from this, all I feel is bliss. Total bliss.

This gift could be yours. Before you continue, consider this: most people are searching for something, and when it comes down to it, the majority of responses would be to find happiness. However, very few people find anything that remotely feels like happiness or approaches contentment in their lives. They turn to television, cinema, theatre, sports, and other forms of entertainment, which may satisfy their needs for a short time, so they seek material possessions, constantly spending their recreational time in retail therapy buying unnecessary things that clutter their home.

Yet lasting happiness seems to elude them. In return for their effort, they experience feelings of insecurity, jealously, envy, hatred, fear, and anger. Left unattended, these emotions can develop in the physical body and present themselves as liver disease, kidney disorders, diabetes, heart conditions, and cancer. In the mental body, depression may be the first symptom. Did you know the two most-purchased items worldwide last year were antidepressants and self-help literature? What does this suggest about the current tend in the quest for happiness?

The path towards contentment in life, love, joy, and exuberance is so simple. My journey from darkness to light is an example of this. Initially I was forced to address the physical pain experienced in my body. With assistance from natural treatments, medical advice, and pharmaceutical drugs, I was unable to alleviate the symptoms. This created feelings of anxiety and rage. Appealing to the physical body alone was ineffective. Being a yogi, I have the skills and knowledge to treat pain through asanas and pranayama yoga, but something else was needed. I was yet to find the cause of my suffering.

What I hope to share with you is my journey from despair to hope, from ignorance to knowledge, and knowledge to wisdom. How did I do this? Let me tell you my story. I'm not suggesting my path has all the answers, hence written in stone. The works of great sages, gurus, and yogis alike have their work written in stone. This information has been passed down over the years and their theories and concepts remain the same. Yoga will brighten and expand your life. If you are willing to be open and honest, the light will spread to all aspects of your life. It will remove obstacles and blockages to release healthy and positive emotions. It has the potential to open the doors to self-discovery and possibly the ability to transform and create your life. *Insights of a Yogi* is a detailed account of my experience to freedom and liberation, and I was able to achieve this through the ancient holistic science of yoga. Your life can be full of hope and optimism too. Simply read on.

INTRODUCTION

The structure of the book is unusual and sometimes unexpected, with the text changing from a personal account and writing in the first person to an analytical review of yogic literature and research papers. Unconventional perhaps, but this was deliberate and very much my intention. In its true essence, my book is devoted to yoga and the philosophical aspect of yoga. When discussing the yoga sutras or the Bhagavad Gita, the topics can be complex and confusing. Even studying for three years under the supervision of highly versed and knowledgeable teachers at the ashram, I still found it gruelling and perplexing. In appreciation of this, I have structured the book in such a way that I hope helps bridge the divide. By calling upon my own experience to demonstrate some key points or issues, I hope to bring some insight into these areas of concern.

There are seven chapters, and each one has been dedicated to the seven chakras of the body. Each chakra has key characteristics that define the energy centre and themes that exist within that energy vortex. I have tried to explain the significant factors pertaining to each chakra, using my life as an example and ways in which I have either healed or unblocked negative energy or emotions that were causing pain or suffering in my life. I offer yogic practices, specific to each chakra in each chapter, so the book can also serve as a guide. These are my insights from years of practising and studying yoga that I hope you will find useful. My dedication to yoga and my persistence to practice have given me direction and purpose in life that I hope to share with you.

CHAPTER 1

Mooladhara

Finding Your Feet

From the moment we take our first step, we are finding our feet. Stressful as it may be for our parents to watch the unsteady show, it is the beginning of a new independence for the children, finding freedom in every step to search places beyond their wildest dreams. Like the old adage, "Every journey begins with a single step," we too are on the road to life. The journey through the chakras begins with the base, or root chakra, known as mooladhara.

Mooladhara is the energy centre that controls the "will to live," our survival instincts manifesting in our fight-or-flight response. Our earliest experiences, including the extent to which our basic needs are met are recorded here whether consciously or unconsciously. These impressions are stored on our body's "flash drive," and depending on our life experiences, they have an impact on our sense of security and belonging.

Strangers took me from school when I was five. Like any other day, I was walking out the front gate on my way home, when suddenly I was shoved into a car. We drove for a short length of time before arriving at an unfamiliar address. I had no idea where I was and who the people were. For three days I sat, slept, and ate with my captors. By no means were they unkind. The whole situation was, however, uncomfortable and very unpleasant. I missed my family.

Unbeknownst to me, my parents (in particular my mother) was miserable with her life and in her desperation had staged the kidnapping. My mother was very young when she became pregnant. With few options available, she moved into my father's parents' home until I was born. At the time, my father owned a successful café in Sydney and spent most of his time at work. Their marriage was fraught with hardship and sadness, and it was not uncommon for Mum to be heavy with depression. Unsure how to leave my father, she felt it best to do it discreetly and consequently organised strangers to take me from school.

On the day of the kidnapping, my father returned home from work only to find the house empty. He must have assumed no harm was caused because everything had been left neat and tidy.

But after months of separation, heartache and pain, Dad hired a private investigator to find us. An extensive and desperate search ensued. We were difficult to locate, as Mum had changed our surname and address, plus we had moved to a remote country town.

It took eight months for my father to find me. I will never forget that time. Men in suits raided our home in the middle of the night. My father was one of those men. His eyes were painfully sad when he first saw me. He tried hard to hold back the tears. That was the beginning of an ugly court case. At the conclusion of the trial, I was nine years old. Even though nasty things were said and accusations were made, my mother was awarded custody.

The Role of the Family

The role of the family is to provide essential needs like food, water, clothing, and shelter as well as love, acceptance, and security. How well the family performs these roles will determine many social outcomes in life and can influence personality and behaviour.

I can't determine one moment that shaped my life. It was difficult to trust and believe in adults, especially after the kidnapping and court case. I was teased at school for many things but mainly for having a "snotty nose," not wearing a school uniform, and for being the owner of "strange" but healthy food in my lunchbox. I was punished for being at school early and was often locked in the storeroom at lunchtime. In my mother's defence, she felt handkerchiefs were dirty. She had no money to buy a school uniform and was a strong advocate for healthy and nutritious foods. Furthermore, she had no choice but to take me to school early each day due to her work commitments. The headmaster had no reason to isolate me from the other children—she just did.

Always in the spotlight, was I a victim of circumstance—or was this the beginning of a victim mentality? During the years that followed, we continued to use the false name and live in a small country town.

I was introduced to a man who later becomes a negative influence in my life. He was a friend of the family and I refer to him as my childhood abuser. Over the years this man's actions become inappropriate and violent. His moods were inconsistent and unpredictable by nature. It was not uncommon for me to fear for my life. For example, for sport, he used to load a shotgun with matchsticks and hunt me down like an animal in our enclosed backyard. Sometimes cornered, with my back against the wall, he would shoot directly at me. It always felt final. He must have enjoyed the unbridled fear in my eyes. The matchstick bullets really hurt. I was whipped and beaten with a leather strap for eating grapes on the sofa. I was scrubbed until red and raw for being "dirty" as a child. I have so many examples of abuse and mistreatment by this one fellow, most of which was not known by my mother. He was capable of performing acts of indecency and cruelty. I have spent most of my adult life tormented by my past.

Strangely, this was not the first time I have been subjugated to the whims of this man. We have shared a past life.

Interestingly, one of the archetypes associated with the root chakra is the victim. When feeding the victim mentality, you allow yourself to become vulnerable, needy, and fragile. Every disappointment, separation, or loss is regarded as a direct attack on your soul. To mask the disappointment of my needs not being met as a child, I drank heavily as a teenager. Comparably harmless behaviour when you consider the options available for people wishing to escape their world, but nonetheless, I was good at it.

Conversely, during this time my mother and I became very close. We formed an alliance that became our bond. The functional side of this archetype is the Earth Mother, which is universally associated with nourishment, caring, and unconditional love. In her gentle and passive way, my mother provided physical essentials like a home and food and psychological essentials like love and humour.

Despite my background, I excelled at sports and school. I represented the town and district in netball, basketball, and other athletics. I came first in my year in physical education, third in mathematics, seventh in science, and so on. I was school captain twice and sports captain three times. I was painfully good at everything I attempted, except for fist fighting (I received two black eyes and a smashed nose for being good at taking boyfriends). In all the years I played sports, I never considered the possibility of spinal injury and losing my ability to walk. I never connected my childhood experiences to breaking my back and unresolved issues relating to my root chakra, mooladhara.

On the Yoga Mat

The sun was shining; it was a beautiful summer morning, the beginning of a new week. The theme for the five-week block was "Less Stress, Relax More," so the students were studying the postures that directly affect the spine and the central nervous system. It was the second round of Surya Namaskara (Sun Salute), and whilst in ashwa sanchalanasana (equestrian pose) I felt a rip or tear in my back. I knew right away it wasn't good. We finished the round and I continued to teach the class. When it came to backbends and whilst in dhanurasana (bow pose), I was surprised I couldn't do it. My back just would not bend. I started to sweat from worry and after a very rushed yoga relaxation, I raced into the house to consume a handful of painkillers.

By midafternoon the pain was intolerable, so I rang my doctor. His first response was, "What are we going to do with this back of yours?"

This was not the first time. Over the past twelve months I had been on his doorstep with complaints, concerns, and frustrations. I told him this was different, maybe a new injury. "It really hurts, and I can't sit down," I sobbed.

He prescribed strong pain relievers and asked me to report back in a few days.

In situations like these, I felt a second opinion couldn't hurt, so I made an appointment with a general practitioner who is also a practicing swami in the Satyananda tradition (a type of yoga practice). Unfortunately, my medical history was too long and detailed for any one person to comprehend, so it was decided to adhere to bed rest and take pain medication when required.

The following morning it was time to organize my three children for school, but I was unable to move my legs. I was paralysed from the waist down. My brain was commanding the action, but there was no motor neuron response in the limbs. In shock and unsure of what to do, my husband called an ambulance. I didn't know whether my case was worthy of such attention, but before I could argue I was taken to hospital.

On arrival, a team of attending doctors took a brief case history and it was decided I had a serious case of sciatica. Rest and pain relief were prescribed. Just before leaving, the supervising doctor reviewed my case and performed some neurological tests.

I must have caught his attention with a ridiculous smile across my face. Odd really when in so much pain. He took a closer look and said, "What are you doing here?" Imagine my surprise when I recognised him. After our greetings, I explained my situation and spoke of the ripping feeling in my back I'd experienced whilst teaching yoga. He left to make a few phone calls. Within minutes he had organized a bed at a private hospital so the leading spine specialist could review my case. It's nice to have yoga friends on and off the mat. I was most fortunate that my friend was working in the emergency room on the day of my injury.

I must admit that my time in the hospital was easier than expected. I thought I would be emotionally torn by not being available to my young family. They were so little and didn't really understand the gravity of the situation. The joke was, "Which one of you stepped on the crack and broke your momma's back?" My family came to visit every day and the time passed quickly. During my stay, an MRI was arranged to determine the physiological cause of the pain. Before the results were available, I decided to go home and resume teaching classes on that Monday. My discharge notice read that it was preferable for me to remain in the care of the doctor and maintain bed rest, but I was a determined young lady and chose to go home.

A few days later, I met with the spine care specialist, and he reviewed the results from the MRI. There was a large broad-based bulge at the L4-L5 disc indenting the thecal sac centrally, which means I had a bulge on a disc in my spine placing pressure on my spinal cord.

It can't be that bad, I thought, *as I am walking and teaching classes this week.*

The doctor confirmed this when he said I was "lucky." Phew! Lucky! Apparently the injury occurred only millimetres away from what would have otherwise resulted in spinal surgery.

"A sneeze or sudden movement," he said, "will have you on the operating table. And by the way, yoga is out of the question."

He strongly advised me to find a new career. *This can't be true! I have studied and trained too hard to just stop.* My husband spent the last two years building my yoga studio to conduct my classes. I couldn't just stop! All my dreams, hopes, and passions had been working towards this point. Now that I'd arrived—managing a successful business, doing what I love—I would have to stop because of the imminent risk to my spine and general health? I walked away devastated. Emphasis on *walked*!

Back to Basics

I was no stranger to exercise. I managed successful fitness centres in Sydney and competed in triathlons, particularly the Saucony and Brooks short distance series. In preparation for a competition, I would train up to twenty hours per week. One of the hardest events I ever entered was a swim across Darling Harbour. The distance was achievable, but what was in the water was terrifying. With each stroke my arm came in contact with debris and trash. Anyway, that was what I was hoping for and not the alternative— blue bottles, stingrays, or even sharks!

My first yoga class was after this swim. I thoroughly enjoyed the class and decided to attend weekly. The postures improved my general health and enhanced my fitness training. It wasn't until the birth of my twins that I really immersed myself in yoga. I would practise every day in front of the television. I had an extensive video library covering different aspects of yoga, but I was already familiar with Iyengar yoga and wished to continue with this style. The fitness centre where I was employed was desperate for a yoga teacher and suggested I take a class. Coupled with my inexperience in teaching yoga at the time with my lack of knowledge, I was apprehensive and extremely nervous about the prospect. Twelve years later I still teach yoga at the same centre, and many of the students who witnessed my first class still attend today.

I have always had an unquenchable thirst for knowledge, and now that I had a regular teaching appointment, I wanted to know more. I rang the ashram at Mangrove Mountain and spoke to the head of education. In our conversation, I expressed my desire to study yoga, as I felt after years of practising I knew nothing.

He said, "I know what you mean. I have been studying and teaching yoga for thirty years and feel like I know nothing." This was the beginning of a beautiful friendship with an amazing man and yogi but also the undertaking of a three-year diploma in Satyananda yoga.

Living in an ashram sorts out those who really want to embark on a yogic journey with those who are not sure. The study of asanas, pranayama, and meditation is a major part of the experience, but the complete surrender to expectations and desired outcomes is the hardest aspect of the learning. The day begins with the singing alarm (an alarm clock that plays yoga music) at five in the morning to prepare the students for morning practice. After breakfast, which is consumed in silence, you are assigned a task. I was assigned to clean the men's toilets. Ironically, I had a house cleaner and hadn't been near a toilet bowl with a toilet brush for the last two years. Needless to say, I wasn't thrilled with the prospect, especially after lagoo (a saltwater intestinal wash)—until I had to build a road out of heavy stones in forty-degree heat.

By the end of the first day I was exhausted. All I wanted to do was to retreat to the river for a swim. Instead, I was asked to clean the kitchen and mop the dining hall. After dinner and clean-up, the students assemble in the sadhana hall for kirtan (chanting). Exhausted by the daily activities and studies, it's easy to fall into bed for a good night's sleep.

During the days that followed, a number of students resigned from the course, realising this path was not for them. I was also hanging on by a thread. Morning practice did not concern me, nor the physical aspect of ashram living. The torment for me was the separation from my babies. I had three children younger than age two, and here I was pursuing my passion to learn yoga at the expense of my family's needs. I had to find a solution to my problem. So after kirtan, I would jump in my car and drive for two hours to be home in time to tuck my babies into bed. I would then set the alarm for 3:00 a.m. to wake in time for morning class at the ashram. I did this for three years. One morning my teacher asked if there was something I would like to tell her. "No, no!" was my response. They knew. It was hard not to. The headlights of my car pierced the sadhana (study) hall every morning and I always fell asleep during nidra (relaxation).

At the ashram, your commitment to yoga and to yourself is tested. This is part of the journey. In the last year you are required to undertake teacher training. By now I had been teaching for several years and felt comfortable in front of fellow students. When the time came for assessment, I had to discuss the format with my supervisor. We sat under a flowering Alstonville, embracing the energy of the morning sun and the prana from the trees. We were alive with life and ideas and decided to chant the mantras to each asana in Surya Namaskara (Sun Salutation). To complement the practice, we decided to do Ajapa Dharana (repetition and concentration) and Soham mantra (natural sound of the breath) to invite the vibration into every cell of the body. The class was to finish with a meditation to awaken the senses. My confidence had never been strong when singing in public. I don't know how bad my voice is—I just know it's bad. So to chant the mantras in sequence to the asanas was a test of my ability and self-confidence.

I woke early on the morning of my assessment to prepare the fire in the sadhana hall, vacuum the floor, and fold the blankets. I even turned to Swamiji (1960–present, the present head of Satyananda Yoga and founder of Bihar Yoga Bharati in India) on the wall and asked for his help and guidance. I needed all the support I could muster.

To my surprise the class went exceptionally well. The mantras were chanted with so much energy and effort that I was tingling from head to toe. Fellow students made similar comments after the class. I felt so alive and invigorated that nothing could spoil my day.

However, my supervisor decided to withhold my grade because he felt my teaching skills needed attention. In complete disbelief I argued for hours, trying to uncover why he felt this way. Nothing was concrete, but he said there were some timing discrepancies. Apparently I hadn't allowed sixteen seconds between postures. Okay, a little hard to swallow, but I took this into consideration.

The next day another student was being assessed. Unfortunately, the mantras were not in sequence with the poses and mistakes were made throughout the whole practice. I am not being critical or egotistical by any means, as teacher training is a perfect opportunity to demonstrate your skills in a safe and nurturing environment. During the morning review, her errors were noted yet the student was awarded a pass.

Normally a person who refrains from public displays of emotion, I was surprised by my reaction. First were the tears, hot and moist, initially swelling in my eyes until I was unable to contain them. They came in buckets, rolling down my cheeks, pooling into my lap. Then I felt the heaviness of sadness settle in and the curse of depression consume me. This was beyond comprehension. Why was I so affected? It simply didn't make sense.

I decided to speak to the year coordinator. During our meeting, she explained that my supervisor was also embarking on a learning journey as a teacher and asked if I could show some compassion. Another okay. But I still hadn't passed. I cried so many tears for one week. I was so sad. My sorrow ran deep. My existence felt hollow and incomplete. No words could console my broken heart. I lived and breathed yoga. Everything I had ever known and wanted was to be a yoga teacher.

I approached the head of education, my initial point of contact at the ashram. We spoke at great length, and he commended me as a student teacher and confessed the guidelines for my assessment were more stringent compared to others. This was difficult to digest, but I was left with this concept. It later occurred to me that this was not about my ability to teach, as I had already been offered a position to teach at the ashram. This was part of my spiritual journey. I was being asked to look deep into my soul and ask the question.

Forced to Look Deeper

When you are forced to look deeper into the layers of your conscious mind, all is revealed. The pettiness and conflict that troubled your thoughts cease to be important. You still live and interact in the world, undertaking your duties, but you feel a continual state of contentment. You come in contact with that which has meaning and that which does not. All superficialities that previously consumed your thoughts fade and eventually disappear from the mind. There was more to myself than I had known, but in the wisdom of my mentor, the lesson was not to do with my credibility as a teacher but my credibility to myself.

On the Path

I hesitated to book into an Ashtanga (a style of yoga codified and popularized by yoga teacher K. Pattabhi Jois) weekend workshop with Manju Jois, the grandson of Pattabhi Jois, as my back was constantly sore. I was more concerned about the primary series, as this involves forward bends. I had noted that forward bends, particularly the seated ones, aggravated my condition. However, I wanted to work through the second series with the great master and decided to book my place. Before each session, I loaded my system with paracetamol (an over-the-counter acetaminophen) so I could train without pain. At the end of the workshop I asked the teacher why I was experiencing so much pain in the transition from urdhva mukha svanasana (upward dog) into adho mukha svanasana (downward dog).

After some consideration, he said, "As we age, we have to customize our practice."

This is true. I took this onboard, as the impact of yoga is never purely physical. In the words of B. K. S. Iyengar, "Asanas, if practised correctly, bridge the divide between the physical and mental spheres. The primary aim of yoga is to restore the mind to simplicity, peace, and poise and to free it from confusion and distress."

This notion was reinforced in an anatomy and physiology course I undertook, when the teacher stated, "The rewards of asana are undoubtedly flexibility, strength, endurance, and stamina, but the practice of yoga will lead you to your life's purpose."

Whilst studying yoga under a senior Iyengar teacher in Byron Bay, I recall a comment he made: "When you are closer to your truth, there is less conflict and confusion in life." Powerful words indeed, and to this day they still resonate.

Lost along the Way

It is said that the practice of yoga integrates the body and mind, the intelligence, and finally the self. Yoga offers the skills and knowledge to achieve emancipation and self-realisation, which is the ultimate goal of every person. Unfortunately, I am a slow learner and found it difficult to accept that a once-supple yet strong body could be experiencing so much pain.

There was no apparent or medical reason why my back was riddled with pain. My doctor ordered an X-ray so more could be revealed. As soon as I was on the table, the radiologist said, "I can see a predominated disc bulge at L5." In conclusion, there were several disc bulges proximate to nerve roots and associated with exit foraminal narrowing, but at this stage there was no disc material compressing on nerve roots.

This explained some of my discomfort. My yoga teacher told me disc bulges are quite common. So I decided to investigate the workings of the lower back, in relation to back pain and how these relate to yoga. Here are my findings.

The Source of Back Pain

Physical inactivity among the Australian population is now widespread. Four national surveillance programs (NHMRC 1996) have documented that approximately one in four adults lead sedentary lifestyles, with little or no physical activity. Prevalence of inactivity varies by age, ethnicity, and geographic region, but there is a common theme underpinning the current situation: the lack of physical activity and the burden of health risks rests most heavily on the least active.

In addition to its powerful impact on the cardiovascular system, physical inactivity is also associated with other adverse health issues including osteoporosis, diabetes, cancer, and back pain. My main area of concern is the relationship between back pain and physical inactivity, arising from a sedentary lifestyle. Furthermore, I am interested in the effects of pain on the body, particularly the spine, as this was my experience, but I was also interested in the management of back pain through yogic practices.

Certain careers and professions require little physical activity, as most work is done seated at a desk in front of a computer over long periods of time. Commuting to and from work is usually done in uncomfortable and ill-equipped seats. In an attempt to relax, many choose to lounge in front of the television. With poor or incorrect alignment of the spine day in and day out, coupled with less time spent on leisure activities, sports, or fitness programs, the health of the lumbar spine is compromised.

Pain is often the first indication the lower back is in trouble. When the muscles surrounding and supporting the spinal column are held rigidly and uncomfortably contract over time, pain or discomfort arises. The muscles tend to go into spasms, and as a result, "fibroblasts" (a type of <u>cell</u> that synthesizes collagen and plays a critical role in wound healing) infiltrate the area, laying down fibrous tissue. The fibrous tissue forms nodules, or bands, within muscle, which block or limit the natural flow of blood and nutrients to the area. As a result, the lower-back muscles lose tone and flexibility, which contributes to functional inadequacy of the spine.

View of a healthy spine

In a healthy body, the lumbar spine is a flexible, segmented structure at the base and immediately above the sacrum and coccyx. There are five lumbar vertebrae in the lumbar spine, which are larger in size and designed to bear the weight of the bony structures positioned above it. There is a natural curve, or lordosis, in the lumbar also designed to bear weight. The intervertebral discs are the thickest in the lumbar area, also providing strength and stability but allowing movement throughout the spine. Where the vertebrae provide the stability, the intervertebral discs provide the shock absorption and mobility. Facet joints hook the vertebrae together to provide security, and as such are the ultimate reinforcement to the spine. They are like the scaffolding on a building site.

The structures of the spine form a highly sophisticated system that communicates information to the nervous system. Vigilant and attentive to the needs of the body, the role of the nervous system is to keep the body up to date about the position and health of the spine.

Depending on the muscles used, each vertebra can be made to move in a variety of directions: lateral flexion by moving sideways as in trikonasana (triangle pose) or forward flexion, as in paschimottanasana (seated forward bend).

Trikonasana, Pascimottanasana and Backbends, as in Ushtrasana (camel pose), create space between each vertebra.

This is how the spine achieves phenomenal range of movement, enabling the possibility of touching the nose with the toes in poorna salabhasana (full locust pose) or vrischikasana (scorpion pose). As mentioned earlier, the demise of the lower back is when the space between each vertebra is lost. This could be as simple as physical inactivity over time and/or extended periods of sitting. Over time the discs lose height, and as a result, the vertebral bones become closer to each other. The more compressed the spine, the less it can absorb shock, hence it becomes more susceptible to injury. If the disc were to dry out and drop in stature, the super-incumbent weight of the body bears down on the weakened disc wall, causing the discs to bulge flaccidly under pressure, hence the workings of a herniated disc. The fluid that seeps from a herniated disc is like air leaching out of a car tyre. In turn, the facet joints start to grind, becoming swollen and inflamed. A source of severe lower-back pain results due to the lack of space between the structures.

The natural and most effective way to reduce the incidence of disc shrinkage is through exercise. By performing movement or physical activity, the discs have an opportunity to replenish the fluid required for healthy functioning. Furthermore, exercises or movement that encourages spinal elongation can even assist a lower-back problem already in evidence.

A simple and effective way to incorporate physical activity for the purpose of optimum health and well-being can be found in yoga. Gentle on joints, forgiving on injuries, and deeply relaxing, yoga is for everyone. To practise yoga you need not be at the peak of physical fitness as there are yogic practices to suit everyone. When done regularly, yoga has the ability to correct poor spinal alignment and improve muscle imbalance and weakness by increasing strength and flexibility.

Generally speaking, postures, or asanas, are extremely beneficial to the whole body, thus having residual benefits for the lower back. Asanas strengthen the bones and muscles, correct posture, improve breathing, and increase energy. It is also known that yoga improves the functioning of the respiratory, circulatory, digestive, and endocrine systems by increasing the supply of fresh blood supply to all vital organs and assisting in the removal of toxins from the body. Regular practices of stretches, twists, bends, and inversions help restore strength and stamina plus assist in body alignment.

Standing practices such as samakonasana (right angle pose), tadasana (mountain pose), tiryaka tadasana (swinging palm tree), kati chakrasana (waist rotation pose), and the trikonasana (extended triangle pose) series correct poor body alignment by straightening and elongating the spine.

For lengthening the spine, the following seated practices could be included in a session: janu sirsasana (head-to-knee pose), paschimottanasana (seated forward bend), and pada prasar paschimottanasana (legs spread back stretch pose). No doubt these practices can also ease stiffness in the lower back muscles as well as tone the abdominal group.

The vajrasana (thunderbolt pose) series has the foot positioned at 180 degrees, or resting flat on the floor, which is excellent to relieve ankle stiffness and inflexibility. Vajrasana also relieves stiffness in the joints, especially the hips and knees. Pawanmuktasana, part one, the anti-rheumatic group of practices, is excellent for releasing lubricating fluid into the joints or for activating the production of synovial fluid, eliminating energy blocks by the increase in flow of prana and circulation to the area. Pawanmuktasana, part two, is beneficial for strengthening the abdominal muscles and eliminating energy blocks. The shakti bandha asanas are useful for people who lead a sedentary lifestyle as this group eases stiffness in the lower back and replaces it with energy and vitality. Surya Namaskara is an excellent series of practices designed to balance the body by the continual flow of forward and backbends. The sequence also helps stretch the hip flexors (which when tight can cause an anterior tilt to the pelvis, further complicated by weak abdominal muscles that can create lumbar pain or discomfort) and the hamstrings. The versatility and application of surya namaskara make it one of the most useful methods of inducing a healthy and supple body and may lead to higher practices such as spiritual awakening.

Backbends tone and strengthen the muscles that control the spine. Through correct guidance and practice this group of asanas can help prevent herniated discs and other back conditions as well as heal others.

When considering the statistics on back pain, one study concluded that in four out of five patients, acute back pain occurs simply because the functional demand upon the back muscles exceeded capacity (NHMRC 1996). In another report, (Dr W.D Freidman of the I.C.D Rehabilitation and research centre, USA) it was found that there was no connection to back pain due to conditions such as herniated disc, tumours, or organic conditions. In fact, in 81 percent of the cases, the symptoms of back pain arose from muscular discomfort, strain, and stiffness.

These figures are extremely high when you consider a random sample of people. Anywhere up to 80 percent have had back pain. When you remove these statistics from the textbook and apply them to the general yoga class, it is sufficient to say a majority of participants have experienced back pain at one point in their life.

To teach in an environment such as a gym, where the participants come on a casual basis, it is best to keep these statistics in mind. One suggestion would be to begin with gentler practices that minimise risk or injury and gradually move to more involved practices when the group develops and becomes more familiar to the teacher.

Another way to approach this special need area is to design a course that accommodates those with back pain. A market strategy could be adopted to attract participants with special needs as well as health professionals, such as massage therapists, chiropractors, and physiotherapists to recommend the course. By approaching the special area on this level, seeking out participants with similar concerns allows the teacher to plan, adjust, and organise the class appropriately, so each participant receives adequate care and attention required to accommodate the special need. Structured in this way, it provides an opportunity for individuals to develop awareness of their own needs, empowering them to manage back pain through safe and low-risk practices. The maintenance of health and well-being will also be derived, as yoga has a profound effect on the mind and body.

As such, certain yoga practices have the ability to restore the spine to improve health by restoring balance to overused muscles. This can be achieved by stretching and releasing tight, constricted muscles and by strengthening the opposing fascia (connective tissue that surrounds a muscle, group of muscles, blood vessels and nerves). By re-educating the muscles to support and align the spine, fewer injuries will take place, leading to a happier and healthier person.

Life's Lessons

Ignoring the signs, I continued to train with back pain. It was impossible to do balasana (child's pose), halasana (plough pose), sarvangasana (shoulder stand), and postures like paschimottanasana. I was really struggling but not willing to give up. I was asked to teach introduction to ashtanga classes and level-two general-practice classes. The students in level two were quite advanced practitioners, some already teaching. We were studying hanumanasana (monkey pose) plus sideway splits, and I am happy to report that after weeks of preparation I was able to demonstrate the posture to the students.

Due to my unyielding commitment to yoga, it was almost impossible to sit, drive a car, or pick up one of my children for a cuddle. I remember driving home in tears after one of many weekends training with an elite yoga teacher who is also a physiotherapist. If I did not have to pick up my son from a friend's place, I would have driven straight to hospital. To help relieve the pain, a friend offered free Reiki sessions, which helped with the inflammation but not the root cause. I decided to radically change my diet and chose to eat raw food and drink fresh juices. This was quite a commitment from a girl whose parents named a racehorse "Champagne Mish" in her honour.

Once again, my doctor asked if I had any rashes on my skin. Both hands were cracked and dry from what I believed to be a residue of detergents from washing and cleaning. They often bled. When it occurred to my doctor that I might have a condition called ankylosing spondylitis, I jumped up in excitement to show him the rashes on my stomach and lower back.

It appeared I had some of the symptoms, especially the painful joints of the spine. I often said to my husband that my back felt brittle yet rigid, like cement and steel. I was soon to learn that ankylosing spondylitis is a painful and debilitating arthritic condition of the spine. If untreated it can lead to permanent fusing of the spinal column. As ankylosing spondylitis is a systemic rheumatic disease, it can lead to inflammation in other parts of the body, including the joints of the hips, knees, or shoulders. It can also affect the heart, lungs, and kidneys. The exact cause of the condition remains unknown, but research has demonstrated that ankylosing spondylitis tends to be a genetic disorder. Evidence for a possible genetic predisposition to the disease is supported by the findings that a specific human leukocyte antigen (HLA) tissue type called HLA-B27 occurs in about 90 percent of individuals with ankylosing spondylitis. Currently there is no cure for it. There are a variety of drugs available to control the symptoms, including pain, stiffness, and inflammation. Exercise therapy is also considered an important component in the management of pain.

I happen to be a carrier of this specific gene, so to confirm my doctor's suspicion I was sent to hospital for a bone scan. What was found was evidence of vertebral spondylitis within the mid- to lower-lumbar spine. Furthermore, mild-to-moderate bilateral inflammatory sacroilitis was evident on both sides. The sad part was that I knew the outcome of the bone scan but continued to physically push my body to the point where the inflammation created so much pressure on the vertebral disc that I ruptured two of them. This was completely unnecessary. I could have avoided this injury. As a result, postures like paschimottanasana that load the lumbar disc were out of the question.

A Student of Life

This experience has equipped me with the information to educate my students to always listen to the needs of their bodies. That is to be in the moment, to listen, and to understand the complexities of physical, emotional, and mental limitations, and to not rely on past knowledge of what the body can do, as each day is different. Never feel pressure or commitment to come into a posture unless it feels comfortable and safe. I have become more empathetic to student concerns and tend to do fewer adjustments for these very reasons.

Drugs, Rashes, and Alcohol

The rashes on my skin were still a concern, and after a visit to the rheumatologist, my condition was labelled psoriatic arthritis, with inflammation of the sacroiliac joints and spondylolisthesis. I was given a non-steroidal drug called Prexige to treat the symptoms. Relatively new to the market, little was known about the drug. Within a short period of time, I started to experience some unusual side effects. For example, my breasts had tripled in size and my feet were swollen. I couldn't go to the toilet, and I felt angrier than normal. Only after three weeks of taking Prexige, I received a telephone call from the doctor advising me to stop taking it. Not long after, I noticed it was removed from the market.

I was still riddled with pain and struggled with the idea of consuming only fresh foods and green teas and practising yoga twice daily. We were in our fourth year without television and chose not to have the Internet. Every attempt was made to live a clean and healthy lifestyle, yet I had to take so many painkillers and drugs to get through my day. So I stopped taking the drugs and booked into a three-week retreat in an Ayurvedic resort in Sri Lanka.

Natural Therapies

Perhaps the enormity of what I was embarking upon hit me on the flight from Singapore to Colombo. Apart from being one of a few females onboard, I was perhaps the only Australian. However, it was the devastation and ruin of the shops and facilities at the airport that caught my attention. Only weeks before my arrival, the terrorist group Tamil Tigers had left their mark. For this reason I chose a flight that left outside peak times to avoid such attacks, but also to arrive in time for the first day of treatment at the Ayurvedic resort.

Driving through the streets of Colombo, I noticed demonstrations and protests. Gangs of men were walking, pushing, and shoving; they were shouting with raised fists, throwing objects, and rocking cars. For the first time in my life I was worried. I felt selfish and inconsiderate to leave a young family to travel to a country known for terrorist activity. Prior to motherhood I had travelled across Europe, Asia, and Africa as a dutiful Aussie backpacker. In Africa I had a scary experience with local law enforcement in a small town called Katino Melino. This was poor timing on my part. I'd arrived at the Namibian border from Zambia just before 6:00 p.m. without a visa. Before Namibia's independence from South-West Africa in 1990, no travel documents were necessary, only a current passport. However, under the new rule, I needed a visa. I didn't know this and wasn't prepared with the necessary paperwork. Too late in the day to travel back to Zambia, I was stuck in "no man's land." (The space between two countries is called no man's land, and the distance travelled made it impossible to return before the border closed.) With nowhere to go and nowhere to stay, my German travelling companions went into town to find help. Members of the Jehovah's Witness Church came to my aid and kindly offered temporary accommodation. Days turned into weeks, and in a strange twist of fate, the local authority misunderstood the church members' good intentions. Somehow the border officials were under the impression I was trying to enter the country illegally to work as a missionary. So they took my passport. During this time I bathed with crocodiles, canoed with hippopotami, and discovered the delights of malaria. Completely oblivious to the dangers I placed myself in, and the effect it was having on my parents, I continued on for the sake of adventure.

However, travelling to Colombo was different. I had responsibilities to my children and family. When I arrived at the first destination, I thought, *This is the last time I book a holiday on the Internet!* The building was tired and broken. There was rubble and ruin everywhere. For my safety, I was told to stay in the car. I waited one hour. It was already 4:00 a.m. exhausted by the flight and desperate for rest, I must have dozed off. Apparently we travelled a few more hours. When the car finally came to a stop, I hit my head against the window. Startled but awake, I was taken to my room and asked to report to the health centre at 9:00 a.m.

At my first consultation I met with a team of Ayurvedic doctors who not only determined my state of health but also my constitution. According to Ayurveda, everyone is born with a basic constitution and this is genetically determined and remains unaltered during the individual's lifetime. Due to a number of factors such as stress, diet, and exercise, an individual's basic constitution can be affected. This can create an imbalance or impose an influence. In Ayurvedic philosophy, the human body has three constituents, or prakriti, called tridosha, that govern an individual's constitution. These tridosha are vata, pitta, and kapha. The tridosha are said to be the main active forces in the body. They govern its physiological activities, the formation of the body, its maintenance and its destruction. When vata, pitta, and kapha are in a state of equilibrium, the person will be in a healthy state of being.

It was determined that I was more pitta in nature but experiencing a vata influence. In most instances a person who is predominately pitta will be of medium height and build with oily skin prone to pimples. They have a fair complexion that is sensitive to the sun. Their eyes are sharp and penetrating and are either green or hazel in colour. Their hair is soft and thin with the possibility of going bald or grey prematurely. Pitta people are assertive and highly intelligent with good memory and concentration skills; however, they tend to be aggressive, quick to anger, and display explosive bursts of rage due to a lack of patience and tolerance. They have a strong appetite and need regular meals. Bowel movements are regular and when out of sorts, tend to have diarrhoea or gastric conditions. Skin rashes and irritations are more common within the pitta dosha.

Frequently experiencing rashes and skin irritations, I tend to show symptoms of a pitta imbalance. Aspects of my personality worked within the pitta classification, but my appetite has always been poor and I am more inclined to constipation than diarrhoea.

I was asked to report back at 3:00 p.m. to collect my medicine. A routine was established with the consumption of medicine. It started with a tonic at 6:00 a.m., a paste at 9:00 a.m., and a powder at 10:00 a.m. I had a two-person massage every day, where traditional Ayurvedic oils saturated with herbs and healing ingredients were worked deeply into my skin. Then I was escorted to the sun garden for herbal wraps, ointments, and pastes to soothe the skin. At 3:00 p.m., there were more pastes, 4:00 p.m. powders, 5:00 p.m. tonics, and at 9:00 p.m. the mother of all medicine, a herbal tonic that guaranteed success in the bathroom.

All the meals were vegetarian and from traditional Ayurvedic recipes. The doctors scanned the restaurant, ensuring you made healthy choices amongst the healthy choices. Some diets are more controlled than others, especially if you are participating in the panchakarmas.

For the first three days I was feeling fantastic. I could almost do surya namaskara with bent knees. By the fourth day, I had acquired boils the size of cherries all over my back. They were big, sore, and infected. They itched and ached and drove me to distraction.

Every time I passed a doctor in conversation I would flash my bumps, to which the doctor would casually respond, "Ah you're detoxing." In a yoga class, at tai chi, even out on the street, people made the same comment: "Ah, you are detoxing."

How could I be so toxic? I ate only raw food and drank fresh juices. Apparently I was detoxing.

Then one day, the 9:00 p.m. herbal tonic must have kicked in. I was close to the bathroom all day. Without a word of a lie by the fifth visit and yet again passing the size of a doorstopper down the toilet, my skin instantly cleared. Not a single spot appeared on my body, not even a scar to indicate their presence. In the days that followed I found it hard to swallow the medicine. The taste almost made me vomit. I informed the team of doctors, to which they said the vata influence was addressed and it was time to adjust my medicine to suit my prakriti.

What I had experienced at the Ayurvedic resort was a healing. Ayurveda, the "science of life," is a philosophy that covers every aspect of being: food, health, spirit, sex, occupation, and relationships. Ayurveda teaches the individual to live in harmony with the inner self and with external influences. The principle of Ayurveda is that good health stems from a correct balance of different energies and as a holistic science, remedies exist for specific problems and can vary according to each individual.

Back home I wanted to maintain the healthy lifestyle I had adopted in Sri Lanka. I felt fantastic and looked possibly the best I could without plastic surgery. (Just kidding). Being an opportunist I decided to pose for pictures for my website. Whilst seated in lotus position, I asked my husband to adjust my knees so I could bind better and then there was a crack! crack! crack! Colour drained from my husband's face.

He said, "I can't watch you injure yourself again."

To which my response was, "I'm okay; you can take the photo now."

Ignoring the signs once again, I continued to train and teach classes. Not too long in the distant future I arrived at the same place I was before. It was impossible to sit or drive a car, let alone teach. Ironically, at this time I was offered a teaching position at a new mind and body centre. The management had designs on developing a successful holistic haven and wanted to expand their membership base. They ran full-page advertisements promoting the classes with my name splashed across the page in bold print. Here I was, supposedly a much sought-after teacher who had to wear a back brace to teach the class. I was also treating my back with natural herbs and spices including turmeric, ginger, and boswellia, together with extracts of rosemary and olive dry leaf for the relief of pain. I swallowed copious amounts of fish oil tablets to reduce the inflammation. My intentions were to heal naturally.

Unbeknownst to me I had entered an active phase of psoriatic arthritis. Classified as an autoimmune deficiency disease, the condition can go through active phases and remission. Whilst in Sri Lanka, I had experienced the beauty of being in remission. In my mind I had no doubt Ayurvedic medicine would heal my body, and it did because I believed it so strongly. However, back to my normal routine teaching classes, running a health retreat, and finding time to be a mother and wife had challenged my mental strength and in turn raised my stress levels. Constantly under stress, the brain interprets a situation as threatening, and sets the adrenals to work. Messages are sent to the nervous system to mobilize the circulatory system and respiratory system for emergency action. Reserve energy in the body is found diverting from the normal functioning of the body. When the alert stage is over, the body continues to stay in a state of emergency, and the body's reserves become depleted and in time weaken the immune system. In the long term, the over-action of stress-release hormones such as cortisol can deplete the kidneys and adrenals, impairing the ability of the immune system to function properly.

The two adrenal glands sit above the kidneys. There is a common misconception as to where the kidneys are located, but if you can imagine the space half in and half out of the twelfth rib in the back, this is a fair estimation. The adrenals contain two parts: the outer cortex, which produces steroids, and the inner medulla, which is part of the sympathetic nervous system and secretes adrenalin. The outer cortex mainly produces cortisol and aldosterone. (Aldosterone is another steroid responsible for pH balance and blood pressure.) Cortisol production is controlled by the adrenocorticotropic hormone (ACTH), which is released by the pituitary gland at the base of the brain. The pituitary responds to a range of signals to release ACTH, which in turn stimulates cortisol release. This is why it is good to stand on your head. Postures such as sirsasana (headstand) stimulate the pituitary gland, thus balance the endocrine system and the production of steroids.

The levels of cortisol fluctuate during the day in a rhythmic fashion. The highest levels are registered in the morning and lowest levels in the evening. Disruption to the rhythm of cortisol and melatonin in the body is partially responsible for the feeling of jetlag.

My levels of cortisol were depleted due to the incidence of inflammatory substances evident in the blood. I needed a little help, and for this reason, I decided to investigate the effects of stress on the mind and body and how yoga practices can treat such conditions.

The Effects of Stress

We have all experienced the way unrelieved tension results in both mental fatigue and ill physical health. This is not a new phenomenon. The causes of stress have been documented in historical texts, where the sage Patanjali identified the ego, spiritual ignorance, desire, hatred, and attachment to material possessions, factors contributing to stress. In a world where technical and scientific achievements define a modern civilisation, there still remains financial tensions, emotional upheavals, environment pollution, and above all, the feeling of losing control by the speed of events that have increased the stress in daily life. All these factors strain the body, causing nervous tension, which adversely affects the mind, creating feelings of despair and isolation. Each system that supports the normal functioning of the body is also affected, and it is here that I wish to direct my attention.

What Happens When There Is Stress?

As mentioned earlier, the first system in the body that is affected by stress is the central nervous system (CNS), specifically the sympathetic nervous system (SNS), as information from the senses are sent to the SNS.

- Messages are sent to the heart, as it requires more blood, and to the liver, as it requires more glucose.
- The liver creates extra cholesterol to drive the stress response.
- Sodium is retained the same way water can be so we don't dehydrate during the stress response (when running away).
- The balance between sodium and potassium changes due to the depletion of potassium in the body. Without potassium, the body is unable to process ATP (adenosine triphosphate), the supplier of energy in the cells.
- The kidneys are placed under extra strain due to the change in sodium and potassium levels, which places pressure on the immune system.
- The immune system is always vigilant, combating any signs of diseases or infection. Signs such as swollen glands and increased temperature are usually indicate ill health, and prolonged stress can suppress the immune system,

lowering the body's ability to fight infection and resist disease.

- Whilst under constant stress, the digestive system is also affected. Some people overeat due to the sense that "comfort eating" provides or additional food may be required to deal with the stress response. Unfortunately, eating in times of stress, when the digestive system has shut down, overloads the system. Often the food contents are left undigested and as a result rot in the system, which can cause constipation or diarrhoea, diverticulitis or IBS (irritable bowel syndrome) and even bowel cancer, depending on the individual.

- ATP, the supplier of energy in the cells, is affected.

- When under stress, the muscles in the body naturally tense. However, in cases of chronic stress, the muscles remain tense, and as a result muscles can tear, or tight muscles can move joints out of alignment. Tight back muscles can pull the spine out of alignment, causing "subluxation" (when one or more of the bones of your spine move out of position) of the facet joints of the spine. Tight muscles can also restrict the natural supply of blood to an area, causing malnourishment of the muscle, resulting in stagnation of energy, which can result in fibrosis and scar tissue. Very stressed people tend to be inflexible, often accompanied with bad backs, sore necks, and headaches.

- In times of stress, the breath becomes rapid, shallow, and short due to the pressure placed on the diaphragm. The diaphragm is the seat of the intelligence, and the heart is the window to the soul. During stressful situations, the diaphragm becomes taut, and the breathing process is affected. Pranayama practices address this problem by developing elasticity in the diaphragm so that when stretched, it can handle any amount of stress, whether intellectual, emotional, or physical.

- The brain, in particular the hypothalamus, plays a critical role in the body's perception of stress. One role of the hypothalamus is linking the body's nervous system to the endocrine system. These connections help regulate the secretion of hormones into the blood. During stress, the hypothalamus secretes corticotropin-releasing hormones that stimulate the pituitary gland, which initiates a regulated stress response.

- The hippocampus is thought to play an important role in memory formation. During a stressful episode, prior memories can have an influence on enhancing, suppressing, or even generating a stress response. The hippocampus can also be susceptible to damage by chronic stress.

- The spinal cord plays an important role in the stress response. Certain nerves that belong to the sympathetic branch of the central nervous system exit the spinal cord and stimulate the peripheral nerves that engage the major organs and muscles in the body to go into "fight or flight" mode.

In a nutshell, when under stress, your heart pounds faster, muscles tighten, and blood pressure increases. The breath becomes rapid, your memory decreases, and the ability to concentrate is negated. Furthermore, the quality of your thoughts is questionable and emotions may be irrational; for instance, you may feel irritable, angry, or overwhelmed. Over long periods of time you may find behavioural changes such as overeating, drinking to excess, or excessive smoking taking place, changes in sleep patterns, and constant aches and pains in the body. If not managed or treated, it can lead to significant illness and disease. Anxiety disorders can result in depression.

You can't eliminate stress completely from your life, but you can always control the way you respond. By taking control of your thoughts, your emotions, your schedule, your environment, and the way you deal with problems can help manage stress. Relaxation taught in yoga, meditation, and through certain breathing techniques can activate the relaxation response, kicking in the parasympathetic side of the nervous system for "rest and digest" action to take place. For this reason alone, everyone should practise yoga. When sometimes overwhelmed by stress, be reminded of the words of Peter Marshall, who wrote, "When we long for a life without difficulties, remind us that oaks grow strong in contrary winds and diamonds are made under pressure."

Bangers and Mash

Probably the two things I dislike most are bangers and mash! But why not indulge? I wasn't going anywhere. Due to the immensity of my pain and a bout of paralysis, I booked myself into hospital in the hope of seeing the spine specialist. My dad, aunty, husband, and kids watched in amazement as I chewed and swallowed "our great inheritance from the English." Cheesecake for dessert? Again, why not! I was told the specialist was not available until the next day. In the meantime, the residing doctor may visit, so why not tuck into the hospital food?

What happened next was completely unexpected. My X-rays were taken on arrival and subsequently viewed. The in-house physiotherapist noticed a large bony protrusion lodged in my spinal cord. Approximately, two cm in diameter, it was disrupting the muscular and nerve information to my legs, causing paralysis.

In the weeks leading up to this event, I thought it quite natural to use crutches as aids. The strength in my legs gradually deteriorated to the point where I couldn't walk. I still had things to do, so I hired a pair of walking sticks. Many times I had to drive with my hands or left leg as my right leg was completely out of commission. Sometimes after a pose like trikonasana (extended triangle pose), I had to physically move my right leg back into tadasana (mountain pose) with my hands.

Before I had the chance to digest my meal, a team of doctors were prepping me for emergency surgery. On that particular evening the ambulance drivers were on strike, so the hospital staff asked my husband to drive me to Sydney. Within minutes I was dressed in a gown, had a catheter, and had an IV hanging off me. The doctors literally carried me to the car with wires dangling everywhere. The attending doctor closed the door and said, "This is what we do to patients who don't pay their bill!" Funny, we definitely needed humour at that moment.

A team of doctors greeted me at the entrance of the Sydney hospital. Within minutes I was lifted from the wheelchair onto a gurney and then inside an elevator. My last memory was bright lights shining in my eyes and telling the nurse I had eaten bangers and mash only hours ago.

Bulge at L-5 pressing against the spinal column.

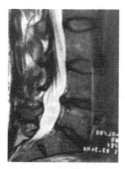

View of the 2 cm fragment wedged into the spinal cord at L-5.

The surgery was successful. A two-centimetre bone fragment was removed from my spinal column. There was extensive nerve damage to my legs due to the spinal injury, and my back was a mess. The disc between L4 and L5 was almost nonexistent, and there was extensive bone damage to the lumbar vertebrae. To help fix the problem, ligaments were removed in a procedure called a laminectomy, and the remainder of the disc was shaved and surgically repaired.

During rehab I basically had to learn to walk again. My brain was instructing my right leg to move, but it would not budge. Nurses came into my room to massage my legs, and I had frequent visits from the physiotherapist. I was incapable of showering (the whole standing thing I suppose), so a gorgeous male nurse had this job. A little weird, like the male midwife I had when my twin babies were born. The length of stay in hospital was determined by my ability to walk again, and the possibility of sex was measured by my capacity to climb twenty stairs, though nineteen would do just fine!

Still Had to Look Deeper

After surgery, I still had to look deeper into the real cause of my pain. I had undertaken the physical path, including rest and gentle exercise as suggested by the surgeon. Yet I was still experiencing pain. The mental anguish was driving me to distraction. Every time I exceeded the exercise prescription and challenged myself physically, I felt pain. Naturally I thought I had hurt myself again. The dialogue was always the same: "Idiot, you have learnt nothing; why are you such a slow learner!"

Whilst doing crane pose, I felt a rip in my lower back. I immediately thought I had torn a disc. I knew something was terribly wrong. Neither doctor nor physiotherapist could convince me I was fine. I was sure I had ruptured the disc again. I wasn't satisfied until I had another MRI. Due to my history and partially because of my personality, the results were rushed. I was advised that everything was fine and healing beautifully. However, this didn't explain the constant feeling of pain. My threshold for pain is pretty high, but this new constant pain was unbearable. It was overwhelming. I wasn't sure if I could survive it.

The pain I was experiencing was due to the minimal space between the vertebrae at L-5 and S1. This is notable in both X-rays. The facet joints were grinding, as seen in the X-ray below. Years later, I underwent a second spinal surgery where spinal spacers were placed between the facet joints to create height and reduce fiction.

 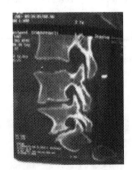

Facet Joints at L3, L4 and L5   **Degeneration at L4 and L5**

The Gatekeeper

A new year had begun with the expectation of teaching classes once again, assuming the healing process would be over. To mask the pain and to perform at the level that was expected of me, I started taking steroids again. This provided me with instant relief. However, over time, my sleep was affected. Starting to feel the wear and tear of compromised sleep, I started taking Temazepam for insomnia. Embarking on a new journey of medication, it wasn't long before I had an almost fatal experience. After copious amounts of chardonnay and a cocktail of medications, I felt myself slipping away. It was early in the evening, and I called the children into the bedroom to say good-bye. I rang my unwell father and asked him to drive two hours so I could bid farewell. My husband was freaking out and asked repeatedly if he should call an ambulance.

Somehow I knew this was different. In the midst of my drug and alcohol fog, I saw a young teenage boy who had crossed over. He was tall and skinny, wearing blue jeans and a T-shirt that hung loosely over his bones. His skin was scarred by acne and he looked beaten. I will never forget his message. He stood outside my bedroom window and said, "Don't go there, and stop mixing drugs with alcohol." My daily cocktail usually consisted of twenty-five mg of Prednisone, one hundred mg of Tramadol, five mg Temazepam, plus wine or champagne to wash it down. I have had visits from the spirit world before, especially when I read as a psychic, but this guy was speaking directly to me. He looked so sad and remorseful.

The force that was pulling me away was so strong, dark, and foreboding. It was almost too easy to slip across to the other side. However, seeing the young man's face and listening to his advice, obviously words from experience, made me change my mind.

When I came to my senses, my whole family was standing in my room. My children were crying, my husband concerned, and my Dad bereft. In the end, I decided not to go with the force. In fact, I was glad to be back.

Not long after this event, I received an interview with a leading doctor and his team at Royal North Shore Hospital to assess my condition. An entire day was spent in the pain clinic meeting with health-care professionals. Being cautious not to sound completely mental, especially in the company of the psychiatrist, I spoke of my mental anguish, always in pain, nurturing the thoughts of despair and failure, in the throes of sadness and depression. I spoke of my meltdown and how I was losing control. After speaking to a physiotherapist and psychotherapist, it was concluded that I had a condition not new to this multidisciplinary team. The pain was real—my brain thought so anyway. Due to the severity of the nerve compression on the spinal column, my brain was receiving information from my body that I still had an injury.

This knowledge alone was therapeutic. It made a huge difference to understanding my mental torture. I felt a huge sense of relief but needed help to deal with the pain. I was given a medication that allows the brain to switch off, offering the mind some peace. Apparently, messages from the nerve sensory were still communicating information to the brain that harm or injury had been caused in the body. However, the medication stops the relay of information from the brain back to the body. This was a nice place to visit.

Unfortunately, it was only temporary. The pain management clinic supervises a programme to assist individuals in the management of their pain. The theory behind the programme is to educate participants on the cause and nature of their pain, and ways to exist within that dynamic. It is their belief the pain will never go away; it is a new constant. This is why it is referred to as "chronic" and therefore needs to be managed, so a normal and satisfying life can follow.

Chronic pain is pain that exists longer than expected. The initial injury or pathology that caused the pain has healed, or the operation has been performed, but severe pain persists for years or a lifetime. Apparently there are two types or chronic pain: nociceptive pain, the processing in the nervous system of noxious stimuli, which is present in clear tissue damage such as arthritis and some types of cancer, and neuropathic pain, caused by nerve damage to the spine or brain.

In his book *Managing Pain*, Professor Cousins states, "Neuropathic Pain is the biggest challenge." He confirms, "Nerve damage, partially prolonged nerve damage, can cause alterations in the wiring of the spinal cord, leaving a memory of pain when the injury has been healed." He concludes that the pain is real, not imagined. A most striking example of neuropathic pain is phantom limb pain. The memory of the pain is captured in the brain even when the limb has been removed.

So little is known about how to treat chronic pain, and this is why so many patients tread the same path over and over again, from bed rest to swallowing painkillers to drugs and alcohol abuse in search of relief.

I was on this treadmill. Initially, I sourced natural ways to assist my recovery. Then I turned to drugs and alcohol. I remember, whilst lying motionless in bed after surgery reading a magazine about healing, an article about an ex-football player who lost the use of his legs. In desperation he flew to America for oxygen therapy, and after six treatments he recovered. I actually rang this guy, spoke in great length about his journey, and decided to undertake oxygen therapy too! (Well, as soon as I could walk and sit in a car.)

The experience was amazing. Not only do you think clearer, you feel lighter. I was so engaged by the treatment that my yoga students drove me to Sydney over the following weeks. Upon one visit, a well-known yogi was using the chamber to practice yoga poses. The chamber is the same size as a body bag and not good for those who are horribly claustrophobic. So you can imagine what poses and funky shapes and beyond my esteemed yogi was bending into.

Included in my healing journey, other than the hyperbaric chamber, were Reiki sessions, massage, visits to Ayurvedic doctors, oil enemas, sweat therapy, and the like. I drank mixtures that tasted like the ash in an ashtray after a big night out. I swallowed potions that smelt like vomit and made me vomit. I got zapped by electric currents until I cried. I rubbed creams that smelt like petrol all over my body and sat under lamps for light therapy. I am not by any means discrediting any of the treatments. In fact, I still drink my vomit and swallow my ash, rub in my petroleum, and get zapped from time to time. I merely wish to express the length I was willing to go to heal and tried to do so by natural means.

After six weeks, I was mentally ready to embark on my normal yoga practice. Sadly, I couldn't even sit cross-legged on the floor. The more I was unable to practice yoga, the less I wanted to. My heart was broken. I could not fathom any likelihood of returning back to a happy, supple body. It was hard as I was still teaching but losing faith every day. I could breathe, chant, and meditate. So instead of feeling miserable and sorry for myself, I decided to practice pranayama everyday, usually a vitalizing, balancing, and tranquilizing style. I would chant the gayatri mantra eleven times; the mahamrityunjaya mantra eleven times; and the Durgas three times. I also practised antar mouna and ajapa dharana meditations. I slowly introduced the pawanmuktasana, series 1, 2, and 3. I began to strengthen my body, particularly the abdominal muscles and lower back, with moola bandha and uddiyana bandha. I slowly introduced walking and set a goal to walk the length of main beach at Hawks Nest. I took Lexi, my mother's King Charles cavalier, for company. I was determined to walk the distance, but Lexi didn't really care about my ambitions. Instead, she dug her paws into the sand and refused to move. My back was too weak to lift the little puppy, so I had to call the lifeguard for assistance. Lexi travelled home in style with the boys, and I walked the rest of the way alone.

Awakening the Sleepy Serpent

Awakening mooladhara, the base chakra, is very important, as it is the seat of kundalini (a sleeping, dormant potential force in the human body). It is important to note that in every human being lives a dormant energy called shakti, and through yogic practices this energy can be awakened. As shakti passes through each chakra, the characteristics and qualities of that chakra are reflected in the individual as behavioural and personality traits.

Not only is mooladhara associated with the "will to live" and "fight and flight," but many emotions are also stored here, such as anger, greed, jealously, hatred, survival, fear, security, and insecurity. People who are unable to shift shakti out of mooladhara may develop emotional disorders like chronic stress and panic attacks. On a physical level, symptoms of a blocked root chakra can be chronic lower-back pain. The most common symptom of an open but blocked mooladhara chakra is that everything is perceived as a crisis or an emergency. Therefore, if mooladhara is blocked or shut down, an individual's life is imbalanced.

Could the constant flip from anger to disappointment in my life be the cause of chronic back pain? Or does it go back to when

I was a small child subjected to physical, emotional, and sexual abuse coupled with being too scared and frightened to speak out about the injustices and mistreatment experienced at such a vulnerable age? This is a time when a child should feel safe and protected, feeling the warmth and security of love and support from a family. A time when you learn how to walk, place equal weight on both feet, and become strong in your legs. This is also the beginning of your emotional journey. It appears disease and illness surface when these areas are not met. It is too obvious to ignore. If feeling overwhelmed by pressure, strain, and stress in your life, or if you have difficulty taking action, consider the following yogic practices to awaken the base chakra and to remove blockages in your life.

Yoga Practices to Heal the Base Chakra

One way to awaken mooladhara is to practise nasikagra drishti, nose-tip gazing. In yoga, the nose represents the spine and the tip of the nose the base or the coccyx. As the eyes move inwards and downwards to sight the nose tip, the mind becomes quiet and focused. There are few distractions, as all external stimuli become less obvious. To come into a balancing posture such as tree pose, you have the ability to stimulate the pineal gland, which is responsible for the production of melatonin, the substance necessary for restful, deep sleep. In conjunction with exercising the pineal gland, nose-tip gazing assists in the activation of the relaxation response by shifting from the sympathetic nervous system, the fight-or-flight response, to the parasympathetic nervous system.

The tip of the nose also relates to the sensory cortex, hence mooladhara is related to the sense of smell. It is said if you practice nasikagra drishti, the muscles of the pelvic floor are stimulated, which assists in the practice of moola bundha. A bundha is a contraction of two opposing muscles surrounding a joint. I can imagine this gives relief to people who have been in search of their pelvic floor muscles for centuries. You can now look directly at your nose tip!

Moola Bundha is one of the first energetic locks we learn to practise in yoga. *Yoga Journal* recently described the bundha as such: "On a physical level, mula bundha consists of a contraction, a muscular lifting-up in the floor of the pelvis. Although the pelvis itself is primarily a bony structure supported with ligaments, the pelvic floor consists of muscle fibres and fascia (connective tissue). These tissues intersect and overlap in complex ways." B. K. S. Iyengar defines moola bundha more simply: he summarizes it as "a posture where the body from the anus to the navel is contracted and lifted up towards the spine." It is not an easy practice to do on the first try, but give it a go!

Moola Bundha

- Sit in a comfortable position.
- Inhale, and at the end of the inhalation, contract the muscles at the pelvic floor.
- Draw the muscles upward, feel the internal vacuum assist in the lift.
- Hold your breath as long as comfortable.
- Release and breathe normally.
- Practise a few rounds daily.

A second surgery was performed to insert spinal spacers. Offering space between the facet joints alleviated compression between the vertebrae. I was the one hundredth recipient of the operation in Australia. After the surgery, I returned to the yoga mat for my rehabilitation. Below, the first X-ray shows the spinal spaces, the second the outcome of two years of constant practise.

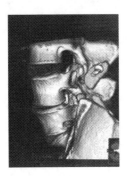 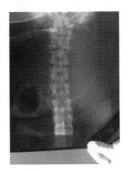

CHAPTER 2

Swadhistana

Understanding Karma through Past-Life Experiences

Have you ever wondered why you had an instant attraction to someone, how when you looked into the person's eyes it was like you had known him or her forever? Or have you had an unexplained fear or phobia for no apparent reason, or more importantly keep making the same mistakes over and over, particularly when it comes to relationships? This chapter should be revealing for you.

The second chakra is the basis of individual human existence. Its counterpart in the brain is the unconscious mind, and it is the storehouse or hard drive of mental imprints and memory. All the karmas, past lives, and one's previous experiences, including personality and behaviour, can be explained here.

The Sanskrit name for the second chakra is *swadhisthana, swa* meaning "one's own," and *adhistana*, meaning "dwelling place" or "place of residence." It is here that past life impressions are stored and these are called samskaras. Samskaras are interesting to say the least. Information from previous life experiences is stored within each and every cell of the body. One cell within the body contains all the data that has accumulated over time. The information is held and stored in our DNA as imprints and are referred to as impressions.

Samskaras are unconscious by nature. It takes time for them to come to the subconscious and conscious levels. When samskaras come to the surface of the mind, they are very powerful. They can manifest in many ways, such as a desire for food, an interest in a hobby, a rejection of an idea, a strong belief, and so on. Sometimes it is hard for the rational mind to recognise an aberration in our personality, a peculiar tendency or trait, or a shift in our thoughts. When an impression arises there is a choice to work with the issue at hand or to ignore it. If impulses are ignored or suppressed, the samskara will bury deep within the unconscious mind.

It is a yogic belief that the practice of yoga will give rise to samskaras. It is the practice of asanas (poses), pranayama, (breath work), meditation, shatkarmas (cleansing practices), and karma yoga that continually work to cleanse and purify the mind and body. The process of inner purification will undoubtedly bring deep-rooted samskaras to the surface of the conscious mind. It is difficult to explain how they manifest and how they will affect personality and behaviour, but tradition suggests ways that yogic practices can assist the process.

Let me explain the concept of samskaras by way of example. I have serious control issues. I am under the impression that I can organise, coordinate, direct, and manage everything better than anyone else, yet I can frustrate a Buddhist monk to distraction with my sense of time and punctuality. Whilst doing a headstand in yoga one day, I had an "ah-ha" moment. You know the feeling when clarity defines all things? As a child, my entire existence was controlled by time and routine. Every moment was accounted for, from the time I woke to the end of the day. I was instructed to serve breakfast, wash up, dust, clean, sweep, vacuum, mop, and take out the rubbish. I had a daily schedule to adhere to, and for years I lived under this regime. I was well aware of the consequences of disobeying the rules. They were harsh and unreasonable. This was a miserable time in my life with very few happy moments. Most of my time was spent riddled in fear, thus explaining my apparent dislike of routines and schedules. I really struggled with this at the ashram, where routine is essential for the program to work. Interestingly, my desire to control events and situations as an adult came from the same experiences as my childhood. As such, there were two distinct behaviours from the one experience. What is notable is how and when they come to surface and whether you choose to acknowledge the information.

According to yogic philosophy, each and every experience, perception, and association is recorded in this life as well as past lives. If you have an argument, a falling out, or a loss, for example, this is registered. If you pass someone in a store, exchange glances, and continue walking, this is registered. Many things come within a range of association. They are not necessarily analysed, but they are recorded somewhere in the recesses of the mind. Daily occurrences and experiences that have seemingly insignificant and unimportant impressions are automatically stored in the conscious mind that forms the total unconscious mind. It is within the unconscious mind that samskaras reside, and yogis believe the practice of yoga can bring them to the surface for the purpose of purification.

Never Smile at a Crocodile

As the song from the children's movie *Peter Pan* suggests, "Never smile at a crocodile; no, you can't get friendly with a crocodile.

Don't be taken in by his friendly grin; he's imagining how well you fit into his skin."

As I sat on the banks of the Zambezi River, I noticed movement in the water. Apparently, a woman had just the other day been taken by a crocodile whilst she washed her clothes. I too needed to wash and bathe in the river, but as you can imagine, I felt a little apprehensive. I had been here for some time. My passport had been confiscated at the border of Namibia, not for any serious offence other than I forgot to organise a visa. With nowhere to go until the documents were processed, I decided to camp alongside the river. So the luxury of bathing and washing was reserved for the great outdoors. Fortunately, there was no evidence of bilharzia—also known as schistosomiasis, microscopic parasites that can bury themselves deep in the pores of the skin and eventually attack the body's immune system in the water. Bilharzia is quite common in Africa, mainly found in still water, lakes, and dams. Their existence can be a serious threat to the intrepid traveller.

As I swung from my hammock day after day, I noticed how the crocodiles moved above and below the water's surface. I watched how one crocodile raised its head to look around. If there were no signs of danger the creature continued to swim, but if conditions were unsavoury, the crocodile disappeared from sight. We are fearful of the incredible power and strength of a crocodile and of their unpredictable nature.

It is no mistake that ancient yogis made the analogy between the nature of a crocodile and samskaras. In traditional yogic symbology, the image of the crocodile is used to display the difference between the conscious and unconscious minds. The movement of the crocodile above or below the water is similar to a past-life issue coming to the surface. If the conditions and situations are favourable, the issue can surface, be acknowledged, and be dealt with as part of the healing journey. However, if an individual feels pain or discomfort with the presentation of an issue or life lesson, he or she has the choice not to deal with it. Perhaps the person is simply not ready and as such prefers to bury the issue deep within the unconscious mind. Therefore, in yoga, the crocodile is the vehicle that carries the whole concept of unconscious life. It symbolizes the subterranean movement of the karmas and information on past-life experiences.

Could My Back Injury Be Related to My Past-Life Experiences?

Absolutely. In my desperation to find a cure for my back injury, I explored the possibility of past-life experiences.

In one meditation

> I saw myself as an Amish girl at the age of nineteen. I was extremely obedient and obliging. I had a close relationship with my father and we lived the Amish life. However, one of the community members was causing concern because he wanted to develop Amish land and more importantly the Amish way of thinking. Initially, he told my father of his romantic intentions towards me and asked for my hand in marriage. Blinded by love, I chose not to follow my father's advice and left with my new husband. Unfortunately, I was a means to an end. His real intention was to acquire my father's land for development and profit. My father sent a message to my new home. The letter was written in the hope to rationalise and eventually discourage my husband from pursuing his grand plan. The news was

not received well. Tempered by anger and rage, my husband picked up an axe and severed the messenger's spine. I watched in shock. From that day onwards, I felt responsible for the messenger's untimely death, not to mention the repulsion I felt towards my husband.

To recall a past-life experience in a meditation practice is a valuable tool. As in my case, it was the catalyst to healing and transformation. By witnessing the emotions and mental torment associated with this particular moment in time was the lesson to be learnt. The significance of the regression was to discover the emotion held in the physical body. For me, that was within the spine. Less importance is placed on the time, as it may take many past lives to reach this one insight. It is the significance of the issue in relation to your life's lesson that is important. Personal growth and transformation can take place in many forms. However, time and time again, I find revisiting past-life experiences through meditation offers the most clarity and distinction to an issue or area of concern.

Forty-Two Birthday Candles

Over the years, I have been placing more and more emphasis on celebrating my birthday. To ensure the day would not be missed, I organised live bands to play on our lawn, booked restaurants, and coordinated massages, facials, pedicures, and the like. The effort I placed on celebrating this one day of the year was extreme. The more I organised, the less folks would come to the party. I constantly felt disappointed and neglected. People would forget to call or send a card. Somehow the day went under the radar.

On my forty-second birthday, I could not contain my grief. I spent hours crying. Hysterical sobbing continued on into the evening, all of which was completely out of character. I had no choice but to research the root cause of my pain to help explain the overwhelming sadness I felt on my birthday. In a meditation practice I saw myself as a young girl of some social standing. I was dressed in a white gown that almost looked bridal, with a floral crown made from frangipanis. The whole village was participating in an event. Men dressed in military uniform lined the streets. My husband in this life was one of those men. It was my nineteenth birthday, and at the time I thought the celebration was in my honour. Unbeknownst to me, the festival was a religious ritual and the sacrifice of three virgins, including this past-life me, to the Greek gods.

This does help explain why the people who are the closest to me resist in celebrating my birthday. Their avoidance is due to the knowledge of my untimely death in a previous life. It also explains my frustration towards my husband, as he was a witness to my death but in my mind did nothing to prevent it. For years I had been angry towards him, as I wanted him to acknowledge my birthday. A card, a flower from the garden, a home-cooked meal, something! But his refusal to do something, anything, was my perception of him not stopping the killings. In saying this, I do acknowledge a part of me was behaving like a martyr.

It is here that the second chakra develops the themes from the first chakra mooladhara, the victim. The idea of martyrdom is self-sacrifice and pity. However, martyrs are less likely to blame external influences than victims, for they perceive life as suffering and the belief that they do not deserve any better. Martyrs also believe nothing is good enough and choose to wallow in self-pity with no motivation to shift or change negative attitudes. It's like the expression, "You get what you expect." Deeply entrenched in this belief is the feeling of scarcity, that there is not enough goodness in the world to be shared by everybody. So martyrs simply miss out. So I whinged and complained about my birthday—until one day I decided to take action. Taking action was "letting go." Simply by acknowledging the pain and trauma and by allowing the issue to come to the surface, I was able to work with it and move on.

Understanding a past karmic event, whether the issue is insignificant, say a birthday, can be monumental and magnificent in your mind, body, and emotions. If not addressed, the issue will continue to surface until it is acknowledged. It took forty-two birth dates to witness, observe, and learn from one past-life experience.

So how does releasing past-life experiences help remove blockages to create miracles in your current existence? What I know is that your thoughts are your reality. For as long as I could remember I wanted to create a healing haven for people to experience the holistic science of yoga and the healing properties of Ayurvedic medicine. I wanted to be surrounded by loving, creative, and nurturing people. Unfortunately, the local council didn't share my dream. They used every tactic, rule, and strategy to close down my retreat. According to the local zoning rules, I was in my right to operate a small business, yet the local council had more muscle than I did. On a weekly basis, I had rangers and sheriffs interrupt classes to deliver foreclosure notices. How embarrassing! Until the day arrived, I continued to operate as normal.

Hours before the official closure, I received a phone call from the town planner. In complete disbelief, he said, "You must have friends in high places. Apparently, the head of land and environment planning has given you permission to continue as normal, and the local council have accepted your application to operate and manage a business."

What did I learn from this? I was so obsessed with someone stealing my dream that I actually made it my reality. I love the story Swami Satyananda tells in his book *Kundalini Tantra*. He speaks of a man who is so thirsty that he wishes for a glass of water, which suddenly materialises. Then he feels a little hot and thinks how nice it would be to feel cool. A beautiful tree appears and provides shade. Feeling hungry, he thinks food would satisfy this need. A meal is presented. Towards the end of the day, the idea of a bed sounds nice. A beautiful bed is made. Then he thinks, *It's very dark, a tiger might eat me.* Exactly.

As you can imagine, working within this domain may require the expertise of a professional or guru to assist you on your journey. In yoga, past-life experience is directly associated to swadhisthana, the second chakra. As mentioned earlier, a chief characteristic of swadhisthana is that it is the basis of individual human existence. It is directly related to the unconscious mind, where all the samskaras reside. The collective unconsciousness, the samskaras, karmas, and past lives, have an impact and influence on an individual's behaviour, attitudes, and reactions. However, not all of these mental impressions are registered on a conscious level. It is possible that an individual may be unaware of them.

As such, an individual may become confused and disturbed by the activation of all the unconscious material. Many negative emotions may surface when shakti (energy) enters swadhisthana. By way of example, a person may become lethargic, depressed, exhausted, and indecisive, thus displaying emotional and sensitive qualities. When swadhisthana chakra is shut down, an individual may have difficulty recognizing feelings, sexual impulses, or creative expressions.

That's what happened to me, but on a physical level. I literately broke my back—well, a piece of my back. I had herniated my L-5 disc so many times that the fluid that is contained within oozed out. The contents solidified and created a hard two-centimetre rock that wedged into my spinal cord. The pain was unbearable. I was taking morphine, prednisone, Tramadol, Temazepam, Methotrexate, and Panadol to ease the discomfort with not a lot of success. My poor liver. I had lost feeling in my right leg, and after three weeks the muscles had deteriorated from poor nerve supply. I was rushed to Sydney for emergency spinal surgery. A team of doctors waited in the parking lot for me on arrival. I was whisked into a wheelchair, rushed through the front doors of the hospital, and positioned onto a gurney. That's the last thing I remember. The surgery went well into the night to remove the broken piece of spine. It took six weeks to learn how to walk again.

During this time, I was still teaching yoga from a chair, and all I could manage was the mantra "OM" at the beginning and end of class. Years later, a traditional Balinese healer said the reason for this experience was due to the speed kundalini, or energy, was moving into my second chakra. Apparently it was moving too fast for my conscious mind to comprehend. So the wedge basically blocked the energy and brought things to a screeching halt.

Swadhisthana is associated with the lower abdomen, influencing genitals and urinary tracts in the physical body and is physiologically related to the prostatic or utero-vaginal plexus of nerves. Due to my injury, I had no nerve information from my bladder to my brain, so I didn't know when my bladder was full. As you can imagine, everything else down there was pretty numb too! I used to jokingly say, "I am too evolved for sex."

To be honest, I knew my reasons for not wanting sex. Time and time again I was called into the bedroom of the man who become my childhood abuser. The walls were painted dark blue. There was a queen-size bed in the middle of the room with cupboards on either side. To the left were mirrors. He would unzip his pants and demand I satisfy him. I was only nine. I remember being at my first high school dance, which happened to fall on Valentine's Day. The boys were racing across the dance floor stealing as many kisses as possible. One boy stuck his tongue down my throat.

I was horrified and yelled out in disgust, "Don't do that, it's like sticking a penis down my throat!" Alarm bells! What was that comment?

Suddenly the teachers and my friends knew something wasn't right at home. Sadly, not much changed over the years. More so, the frequency of the abuse increased. To avoid being physically hurt, whipped, and beaten by a horse crop and shot by a slug gun, I did what I was told.

No wonder I was confused about sex later in life. I was so little when all of this began. I was told I was dirty and got scrubbed raw. Soap was inserted into places it should not go. This man took Polaroid pictures of my body and told me I was deformed. I was so scared that he might show the photos to others. It is very common for victims of sexual abuse to be manipulated by fear. This was true for me, but I chose to repress the feelings, hoping they would go away. I even had the ability to mentally black out when things became threatening or dangerous. Not surprising that my second chakra was blocked and back pain manifested later in life. Issues with L-5 are a direct response to holding on to feelings, especially feelings of betrayal, abandonment, and isolation. It was difficult to trust adults, especially after the kidnapping and years of sexual, mental, and physical abuse. Every time I tried to communicate my situation to another, place my trust in another adult, a similar thing would take place. I was unable to express my feelings and release negative emotions for many years. For these reasons, situations continually surfaced whereby I was a victim of abuse.

I was raped at age nineteen. The rapist came into my room whilst I was asleep at a resort in Fiji. I was woken by the constant thumping on my thighs. Fighting for my life, I kicked and screamed until the perpetrator left through the second-story window. Bruised and sore the next day, I was unable to go swimming, let alone wear a bikini. I knew who it was. He was on holiday with his girlfriend, probably his wife now.

For some time, I was stuck in the past. I obviously had unresolved issues about my childhood that contributed to my sexual dysfunction and lack of interest as an adult. I don't encourage breaking your back to learn your life's lessons but certainly acknowledge the key areas of concern and seek counsel with a professional. Find a healing modality that you feel safe and comfortable with and work through your pain and trauma. Take time to heal and be kind to yourself. I chose the healing properties of yoga. Still to this day I receive the benefits of a regular yoga practise.

Ways to Awaken Swadhisthana

Ways to awaken swadhisthana chakra through the practice of yoga is vajroli and sahajoli mudras, as they rechannel sexual energy. Vajroli is practised by men and sahajoli by women. Asanas that can directly assist the awakening of swadhisthana chakra are bhujangasana (cobra pose) and padahastasana (hand under foot pose), which incidentally are part of surya namaskara (sun salute).

CHAPTER 3

Manipura

When the great warrior Arjuna was in exile, he travelled the length and breadth of India. He came upon Manipura, a mystic kingdom known for its natural beauty. The daughter of King Manipura was also a great warrior and protector of the land. Arjuna was most impressed with her skills as a fighter, especially when he heard about her ability to defend marauders from attacking the village. Not surprising, the reference to spiritual warrior is made when discussing the third chakra in the body. The power of the spiritual warrior lies in inner strength, tempered by the belief that guidance comes from a divine source. This would be true for Arjuna and his relationship with Lord Krishna. His strength was founded and refined by facing obstacles and overcoming challenges. By meeting constant rejection and conflict, the spiritual warrior of myth and legend was forced to look deep within to make sense of situations and circumstance. It is the combination of experience, integrity, and sincerity that leads to growth and development as demonstrated by Arjuna in the Mahabharata, an ancient Indian text.

Manipura, or the third chakra, is derived from the words *mani*, meaning "jewel" and *pura* meaning "city." Hence, Manipura means "city of jewels," or "lustrous gem." It resonates with the colour yellow and is often compared to the life force and energy of the sun. In the same way the sun is the centre of our universe, Manipura is the core or centre for the entire body.

Manipura is located behind the navel on the inner wall of the spinal column. It is associated with personal powers in terms of energetic life force, willpower, determination, and self-esteem. It is also the centre for fire, transformation, and digestion. On a physical level, this chakra is connected to the nervous system, gall bladder, spleen, pancreas, stomach, and the stability of blood vessels.

When people are strong at manipura, they tend to be highly motivated, dynamic, inspirational individuals who radiate good health and energy. They have a strong sense of self-worth that comes from the transformative power of growth and development.

Queen of Fire

Finding inner strength may well be the challenge. It takes a lot of courage to leave the security of a home and relationship. This was the case for my mother. Her situation had become unbearable. Her life had become a living hell. There was no joy or happiness, only fear and misery. She had no choice but to terminate an unhealthy relationship (a relationship after the divorce from my father). Feeling unsure about the future, it must have been a difficult decision. She did, however, have secure employment and a strong network of friends.

When she finally left, our first response was joy. We had been repressed for so many years. We lived in a semi-attached house that had no windows. The carpet and wallpaper were dark and depressing. We were confined to the home, where most of the time was spent doing chores and homework or being forced into an activity against our will. Exploring new possibilities, we booked disco dancing lessons, hosted parties, and went out to dinner. I received a new trampoline and a set of drums. We were having so much fun fulfilling every whim and fancy. We remained on this high for six weeks. Unfortunately, not in a position to finance our newfound freedom, my mother had to find a second job. Her daytime employment was in a psychiatric hospital. I used to visit her work and speak to the patients. I used to think the patients were the sane ones and the crazies were on the outside. In the evenings, she would wait on tables at the local restaurant.

We lived in a small country town, and news of Mum's separation spread quickly. Many suitors came to the door to ask her out on a date. She received gifts of meat (strange, I know). A mechanic fixed the dents in her green Torana. A pilot took her on a helicopter flight. The manager of a fast-food outlet offered her a job and career prospects. These were crazy times, but experience had taught us to be careful and selective, and as a consequence I was very protective of my mother. There were some funny moments, and one in particular stands out; a lovely fellow came to take Mum out to dinner. His name ended in "Smith," and at the time we had a little puppy named Griff—also a gift from an interested suitor. Griff was filled with excitement and joy and was jumping up and down, annoying everyone. Instead of saying, "Sit, Griff," I yelled, "Sit, Smith." He looked so hurt and embarrassed and left without saying good-bye. We burst into uncontrollable laughter. Mum never saw Smith again.

There were also some sad times. One night I came home to find everything in the house had been broken: furniture thrown, plates smashed, mirrors cracked, food scattered everywhere. The worst part was the chunks of hair on the floor and between the rubble. My poor mum. From the look of things, she had certainly put up a good fight. I later learnt it was a jealous ex-wife who caused the damage. She even ran over Griff, who consequently died from internal bleeding.

The jealous ex-wife's behaviour demonstrates an excessive manipura chakra, not the absence of willpower, determination, and energy but the misuse of these qualities.

We survived with very little. Mum and I shared a bedroom, clothes, shoes, and makeup. I had to forego studying at school to secure a job for extra income. However, we were happy. Mum had the courage to take risks, stand apart from the group, and shake off the fear of rejection and criticism to establish confidence and self-respect. These are the qualities that arise from true inner power and a balanced manipura chakra. Years later Mum showed a genuine interest in yoga and decided to test out the ashram. This was during a visit from Swamiji. Only the guru can give you a spiritual name and personal mantra. My mother's spiritual name is Lakini. It suits her. Lakini is the benefactress of all. She has four arms and a dark complexion and radiant body. In yogic symbology, she wears yellow with various jewels and is regarded so highly that she is elevated to the noble position of receiving amrita, which in Hindu philosophy is repeatedly referred to as the drink of the gods that grants them immortality.

The yogic scriptures state that the moon at bindu secretes nectar that falls to Manipura, and when it is full, it sheds its nectar or ambrosial fluid down to permeate the entire body in the same way the moon pours its light over the surface of the earth at the time of its fullness. The flow of nectar produced by bindu makes the body resistant to toxins and strengthens the immune system. In essence, Lakini receives the benefits of wellness and vitality and shows qualities of strength and endurance due to the gift of amrita. Lakini also avoids degeneration and disease due to this bestowal.

Likewise, degeneration, disease, and death can be reversed by the practice of yoga, in particular khechari mudra (curling the tongue towards the tonsils and turning the eyes inwards towards the eyebrow centre), which sends the pranic energy back to the brain. Sirsasana (headstand) and sarvangasana (shoulder stand) release hormones from the pituitary gland into the bloodstream, increasing the flow of amrit. The residual benefits are youthfulness and increased vitality. In addition to the release of hormones, the practices of nauli and trataka are effective when awakening manipura chakra.

Nauli involves abdominal massage through the contraction of rectus abdominal muscles. It is a difficult practice and, according to Swami Satyananda, takes time to perfect. However, when mastered, it activates and regulates samana prana and manipura chakra. Uddiyana Bandha, abdominal contraction, is beneficial for digestive disorders such as indigestion, constipation, intestinal worms, and diabetes, as it improves blood circulation to the area and strengthens all the internal organs.

Uddiyana Bandha

1. Sit in a comfortable position
2. Place the hands on the knees
3. Breathe in deeply through the nose
4. Exhale through the mouth, empty the lungs
5. Hold the breath outside
6. Contract the abdominal muscles inwards and upwards
7. Hold without strain
8. Release the abdominal lock
9. Raise the head then inhale
10. Return back to natural breath
11. Practise 3 to 5 rounds

Uddiyana Bandha

The Sanskrit word for uddiyana means to "lift" or to "rise upward." In the practice, the diaphragm moves upward to the chest. The stomach is also lifted upward. The solar plexus, which has many subtle energies, is stimulated and as a result has the ability to distribute energy and prana throughout the body. Uddiyana bandha must be practiced on an empty stomach, hence best done before breakfast. I am constantly amazed by the results of uddiyana bandha. I see it in my students' eyes. They look calm, relaxed, and content. Their eyes are wide and vibrant and even their skin looks clear.

Since manipura is directly related to digestion, it is suggested to have a healthy and balanced diet. Unfortunately, we live in an era where healthy eating has been negated by food manufactures and convenience, and there is little encouragement to address the body's needs. So often, when feeling fatigued, we ignore the need for rest and manipulate the body with sugar and caffeine. We have lost our ability to relax, and we use drugs and alcohol to find the desired effect. Yoga does offer a healthier solution. By listening to our basic needs, by living according to our body clock and practising pranayama, relaxation, and meditation, we can achieve a healthy mind and body.

In yoga, fasting and dieting are not considered beneficial. From an Ayurvedic point of view, extensive fasting drives the toxins deeper into the organs, tissues, and cells of the body. To fast or diet deprives the body of nutrients, vitamins, and minerals. Furthermore, it weakens the body's constitution, and this has a detrimental effect on manipura.

To remove digestive disorders such as indigestion, hyperacidity, flatulence, constipation, and general sluggishness of the liver and kidneys, the practice of agnisar kriya is not only beneficial but also used as a preparatory practice for uddiyana bandha and nauli. Another shatkarma practice to awaken manipura chakra is trataka.

Trataka

1. Place a candle at eye level
2. Sit in a comfortable position
3. Close the eyes and settle the whole body
4. Open the eyes and gaze steadily at the tip of the wick
5. Avoid blinking and strain
6. When the eyes begin to water after one or two minutes, close them
7. Go within and meditate on the inner images
8. Repeat two to three times

Trataka is excellent practice to clear a troubled mind, for accumulated complexes, and for suppressed thoughts.

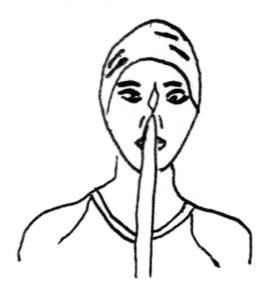

Manipura is directly related to the eyes, and therefore, candlestick gazing can assist in awakening manipura chakra. Naukasana (boat pose) and dhanurasana (bow pose) are specific asanas that can strengthen manipura chakra.

Finding Inner Strength

After separating from her diabolical relationship, Mum received the title to the horrible semi-attached house. Typical of her generous nature, she insisted I have the blue room. I found the courage to tell her why I couldn't accept the offer. So she sold the house. She shared the proceeds of the sale. With my money, I chose to go to Fiji. Not even my mother can protect me from life's lessons.

CHAPTER 4

Anahata

I was instantly attracted to him. He was a friend of a friend and five years my senior, which wouldn't have been a concern but I was late to develop and unremarkable at the age of fifteen. I didn't even register in his thoughts. For the next four years I witnessed him dating girls, some so pretty, others no so pretty. The truth be known he was extremely handsome, hence very popular with the ladies. After completing my final year at school, and before starting university, I took a job in a busy pub at the Rocks in Sydney. It was the hippest joint at the time, and I lied when I said I had experience. I couldn't even pour a beer. At the end of my first shift I got fired. Funny really. So my friend and his mates celebrated my newfound unemployment. We drank copious amounts of champagne, and during the evening, I was approached and asked out on a date. How sweet! From that evening onwards, and after a four-year wait, I had my man.

We were so in love. We did everything together. We even got pregnant. Without his knowledge, I decided to terminate the pregnancy. On the day of the procedure, I woke early and caught a taxi to Surry Hills. There were several anti-abortion protesters outside the clinic with placards and signs. They appeared quite agitated. I felt nervous and scared. At the time I was only nineteen. It was hard to get to the front door because of the crowd. I tend to black out in times of stress and this was no exception. What happened next, I can't really say except a stranger came to my rescue. When I woke and came to my senses, I was lying on a sofa, surrounded by a team of concerned staff. They were under the impression my episode was due to hesitation and uncertainty about the termination. Consequently, a panel of psychiatrists interviewed me and asked many questions. In the end, the procedure went ahead as planned. It was a long day.

After the operation, I felt so empty, isolated, and sad. There was no one waiting to take me home. I didn't know where to go. I hadn't spoken to my mother for more than six months, due to an argument about living arrangements. Feeling broken and wretched, I decided to call her and asked if I could visit. I never spoke about my day and she never asked any questions; instead, we spent the evening watching Deborah Winger and Shirley MacLaine in *Terms of Endearment*.

*

We have now reached anahata chakra, the central chakra within a seven-fold system, the heart of the journey. Anahata, the heart chakra, is characterised by a feeling of universal, unlimited love for all beings. There is no attachment to ego or the self, as actions are guided by complete spiritual compassion. Love is free of expectation. This love is not dependent on others, unlike the tribal love in mooladhara and the sexual love of swadhisthana. Anahata is an enduring and constant state of being. The word *anahata* means "unstuck," or the sound made without "two things striking." It is directly related to the heart, which throbs, beats, and vibrates to a constant unbroken rhythm. It is said in many scriptures that there is a sound that is non-physical, non-empirical, and transcendental in nature. This sound is endless and unbroken from the moment of conception until death. It is the heart. The associated animal archetype for the heart chakra is the antelope, which suggests freedom and love, forgiveness and compassion. Like the creature itself, with its wide doe eyes, restless, wandering, and bounding with joy but always alert, so is the energy centre at anahata.

Hurtful situations can affect or even block this energy centre. Divorce or separation, grief or loss, emotional abuse, abandonment, and adultery can wound the heart chakra. Compassion and forgiveness are required, but it is hard to show compassion and forgiveness to someone who has tormented your soul, whipped and beaten your physical body, sexually interfered with and psychologically abused your thoughts. For many years, I hated the man who severely abused me throughout my childhood.

There are many different kinds of hatred. One type has been passed down by generations due to religious or cultural differences. Strong feelings of hate can stem from unrequited love or heartbreak.

Then there is hatred based on hurt, anger, and resentment. This is what I felt, and it was ugly. It makes you hard, disconnected, fearful, and anxious. It can rot your body, causing conditions like acne, arthritis, and addiction, all of which I experienced. When I was nineteen I had hepatitis, a liver condition. I also suffered from migraines. Both conditions were fuelled by hatred and anger. I was angry for the way this one man had influenced my life, and how I was consumed by it. Seriously, it's not worth it. I used to joke and say, after twenty-six years he probably wouldn't even recognise me.

That day happened. I was teaching a yoga class at the gym when my husband rang. He said, "You are not going to believe this, but a brand-new piano has been delivered to our front door." It was a gift from my mother. My eldest daughter started piano lessons at the age of five, and we were under the impression she had talent. I was so excited that after class I went straight to the music store to purchase sheet music. I was told to wait until the piano expert was available—and then there he was, the man who stole my childhood.

He stood before me, slight in build, grey and distinguished. He asked a few questions in regard to sheet music. Blood drained from my face as I struggled to appear normal. I spoke about my introduction to music. I continued to speak of my experience with playing an instrument, first learning to play the drums, and then percussion and flute. Nothing. No recollection, no acknowledgement to detail, no memory whatsoever. He did not recognise me. Twenty-six years of torment and anguish was for absolutely nothing. I wasn't even part of his conscious thoughts. So what was the point? I could choose to continue to hate and destroy any chance of happiness and well-being, which wasn't serving any purpose, or I could let it go and forgive this man.

What is forgiveness?

Generally, forgiveness is a decision to let go of resentment and thoughts of revenge. It doesn't remove the actions that hurt or upset you but can lessen its hold, enabling you to focus on healthier, more positive aspects of your life. Forgiveness can lead to feelings of understanding, empathy, and compassion. You can forgive the person without excusing the act. Letting go of the bitterness can make room for compassion, kindness, and peace. In the words of Mahatma Gandhi, "The weak can never forgive; forgiveness is the attribute of the strong."

I am particularly moved by Robert Muller's comments on forgiveness, when he said, "To forgive is the highest, most beautiful form of love. In return, you will receive untold peace and happiness." In Nelson Mandela's *Long Walk to Freedom: The Autobiography of Nelson Mandela*, he comments on faith, freedom, love, and hate. From personal experience he wrote, "There are many dark moments that test faith in humanity, [but] no one is born hating another person. ... People learn to hate, and if they can learn to hate, they can be taught to love, for love comes more naturally to the human heart than its opposite."

Love without Expectations

The world is full of contradictions, conflicts, and disappointments. Even if you come in contact with a murderer, paedophile, child smuggler, thief, or drug addict, you have to show compassion and understanding. This may be a difficult concept to grasp, but anahata chakra awakens the emotion within the brain that is characterized by universal love for all beings even when their actions and behaviours are inhuman and selfish.

Nelson Mandela exemplified unlimited love in his quest for antiapartheid, democracy, and reconciliation. Once released from prison, his focus as president of South Africa was to introduce policies that focused on combating poverty and inequality in South Africa. On May 10, 1994, Mandela said, "Let there be justice for all. Let there be peace for all. Let there be work, bread, water, and salt for all. Let each know that for each body, the mind and the soul have been freed to fulfil themselves."

This is a great quest for humanity, to love unconditionally, with absolute resolution. Only a few souls have been able to tackle this feat to date. For many there is the practice of kindness and charity. We do good things everyday to help friends, family, and people in need. So many people are engaged in volunteer work, whether it is for the local school or community, sporting team, or for society as a whole. To give one's time and energy for a good cause is considered an act of charity.

Swami Satyananda describes this as an example of human compassion. However, he stipulates, their charity is not an expression of spiritual charity, which is a prerequisite of anahata chakra. This does pose the question, "What is the difference between the two?" The answer is to remove any expectation of love or reward in return for your efforts. To understand love is free from bargaining or compromise that it is an act of selflessness, which is free of expectation, is the difference between the two.

A New Way of Thinking

It's not easy to change an attitude, especially if you have nurtured it for a long time. So I made the decision to "let go" of my pain and angst towards the man who abused me as a child. Once I did this, things started to change. Firstly, my driving skills seemed less offensive to others. Fewer motorists were honking and sticking their fingers up at me in traffic. Strangers were not so inclined to share their ill-mannered remarks with me. I received fewer insults at the shops. I know this sounds unbelievable, but on a weekly basis people seemed to have grievances with me. On one occasion a complete stranger starting throwing punches at me after a yoga class. I saw him waiting outside the surf club and naturally assumed he was interested in yoga. Quite the contrary. He was under the impression that the sun salute pose was some form of alien worship and wanted to remove their leader. My beautiful yoga students formed a barricade around me to protect me from his swinging arms. The police were called, and this lost soul was taken back to Mandela, an institution for mental health. But why me?

By developing a new way of thinking, and refusing to accept the notion that bad things always happen to me, changed things. In fact, the thought became only good things happen to me. At anahata chakra, the freedom to escape your reality and to create your own destiny becomes a possibility. According to the tantras, there is a tree at the base of anahata called kalpavriksha. It is well known that when the tree comes in bloom, wishes and thoughts come true. Whatever you think or wish for materialises. This may be a hard concept to accept, as up until this point life has been governed by fate.

As there are many wishes to fulfil, priority must be given to the way the wish list is approached. Therefore, the choice of words or attitudes towards your wishes must be clear. For example, you may wish for a new job, but it may not be better than the last. Or you may wish for "that man to go away" and your husband leaves you. Or wish your children to leave you alone, or wish for peace and quiet and find loneliness and isolation. Apparently, if consciousness awakens in anahata and you have negative thoughts, pessimism, apprehensions, doubt, fear, and reservations, you may fall prey to them. To avoid this taking place, Swami Satyananda says you must stay alert, like the archetypal antelope, and listen to every sound.

For much of our journey we have been exploring the elements of the earth, water, and fire, the lower chakras, where you remain completely dependent on what is already mapped out for you, and your fate or karma. The course of fate is real but at anahata chakra one realises the potential to go beyond what fate dictates. In fact, anahata is associated with the ability to make decisions beyond the realms of karma. In the words of Swami Satyananda, "It's like throwing an object into the sky, right out of the gravitational field, where it can no longer be pulled back by the earth's magnetic forces."

So consciousness is accelerated in anahata to the speed of free will in order to transcend the first three chakras. Have you ever heard the expression, "Be careful what you wish for"? Well, this is evident when it comes to the heart chakra. To arrive here is going beyond daydreams and fanciful thinking. It is here that you can navigate your journey, explore free will, and create your future through the process of selective thought.

The Power of Thoughts

Not long after my wedding I wanted to start a family. I know it's a cliché, but my body clock was ticking, and I was already thirty-one. I'd previously had an ectopic pregnancy, and my right fallopian tube was damaged. The doctors told me at the time the chance of getting pregnant was less likely but possible. I honestly believed I was being punished for the termination I'd had at nineteen. For three years it was impossible to become pregnant. I tried everything. I took herbs, swallowed Bach Flower remedies, and had psychic readings, chakra healings, spiritual counselling, and the like. I stood on my head after sex to navigate the sperm in the right direction. At the time, I was teaching at the local high school, and out of nowhere, I rang the head of the department and quit. Just like that. I became pregnant straight after this decision with my first daughter. I wanted a big family and hoped for twins, a boy and a girl. Guess what? The doctors said it was impossible due to the damaged tube. Somehow it healed and I conceived my son on Tuesday and my daughter on Wednesday. Apparently that can happen, where twins can be conceived at different times. So I had three children younger than age two. So be careful for what you wish for and don't have any doubts. Be firm in your knowing and commitment.

Why Do Some People Have Success and Others Misery?

Is it karma? To a degree, the answer is yes, but once at anahata you have the freedom to escape a preordained fate to discover your own destiny. That is the difference. I know this to be true, as earlier this year I broke my wrist. The surgeon had to graft bone from my hip to replace the scaphoid bone in my right wrist. I couldn't wait for the surgery. Sounds weird, but I saw the opportunity to take time out from my busy schedule to rest. Who would do that? My wish was fulfilled; I had time to rest, but a much healthier approach to needing a rest would be to surrender to this need and not try to justify my decision with illness or injury.

How to Awaken the Heart Chakra

The qualities of anahata chakra can be awakened by many methods. One in particular is the practice of ajapa japa. *Japa* means "repetition," or remembering a mantra, and *ajapa* means "constant awareness." Regardless of the mantra you use, the importance is placed on the constant remembrance. The practice helps eliminate the incoming stream of negative thoughts, desires, and emotions. The repetition offers the mind a place of refuge to escape the oscillations. Another important practice in the awakening of anahata is bhramari pranayama, the humming bee breath. The vibrations of bhramari produce a soothing effect on the mind and nervous system.

As music has always been a powerful method for awakening spiritual consciousness, it is my belief that the practice of kirtan, call and response chanting, can assist in the awakening of anahata chakra. One of the great benefits of kirtan is that it can release emotional tensions to bring about a state of tranquillity and peace. Swami Niranjanananda states, "Kirtan becomes the means by which we dive deep into our inner expansiveness." Kirtan is also one of the methods by which bhakti, or transcendental love is awakened, and anahata chakra is the centre of bhakti yoga or devotion. Asanas that affect anahata chakra are dwikonasana, gomukhasana, and trikonasana.

Energy Blocks

If energy is blocked at anahata, a person may experience difficulties with self-love, leaving a feeling of disassociation and perhaps a disconnection with the divine source. A physical symptom could be pain between the shoulder blades, breathing problems, asthma, bronchial infections, lung cancer, blood pressure issues, and/or a heart condition. One way to balance this chakra, other than yoga practices, is to serve others by spending time with someone in need, as a person in a nursing home or a neglected child or animal. Another suggestion is to love and take care of yourself. This could be as simple as a leisurely walk along the beach, taking time to read a book, going to see a movie, or perhaps booking a massage. It may sound ridiculous to "love yourself," or it may feel awkward spending time alone, but it is here that the journey to the higher self begins. Otherwise we tend to stay stuck in the lower chakras.

True Love

It is true, we all crave to love and to be loved. We are, however, sometimes misguided by the greatest love stories of all time, like *Antony and Cleopatra*. Here Shakespeare illustrates raw passion and emotion, whereby no other woman can satisfy Mark Antony like Cleopatra can. In *Romeo and Juliet*, Shakespeare shows the true test of love by the sacrifice of human life in his play. In one of the oldest heart-wrenching classics, *Wuthering Heights* by Emily Bronte, lost love turns a good man evil. Then there is the irresistible attraction between Elizabeth Bennet and Mr. Darcy in Jane Austen's *Pride and Prejudice*. Each tells a story—and we all have a story. Listening to the heart in matters of love is vital to maintaining healthy, mutually respectful, and meaningful relationships. As we embark on our journey towards the higher self, our relationships expose us to what qualities we like in ourselves and in others.

My very first relationship endured many distractions and upheavals. We survived an untimely pregnancy, my years at university, and his employment overseas. There was never any question about our commitment to each other. It was an unspoken promise that one day we would be together. The plan was for me to fly to Japan and get married. I did so well in my last year of studies that I got accepted into New South Wales University to do my master's in education. So I delayed our plans for another year. He stayed on in Japan. Then my dearest girlfriend was planning her overseas pilgrimage to Europe, and at the very last minute I invited myself to travel with her. By this time I owned a fancy sports car, lived in a trendy unit in Double Bay, and had completed my master's degree. I was looking pretty good. The thought of marriage was becoming more of a hindrance than a beautiful union.

The week before my departure, he flew in from Japan, and we spent the whole week in my apartment. It was the most romantic gesture I had ever experienced. Still ambitious to travel, however, I postponed our relationship again and chose to go overseas. I was confident he was the one, so my travel plans were indefinite.

Whilst hitchhiking through Africa, he rang me. How exciting! He invited me to a wedding. I assumed he was speaking of a mutual friend's wedding. There was no way I was allowed to miss this event. My mum had already delivered the speech that I had been away for too long, that it was time to come home, and I had lost the plot. (She actually said a lot more, but the sentence had to stop somewhere.) I naturally thought he was suggesting we should go to the wedding together. At the time of the phone call, I was in a small Namibian town called Swakopmund. I had purposely chosen this destination to protest against the clubbing of seals. I was broke and homeless, spending most nights sleeping in the desert. I didn't care. I felt I was doing something truly important and making a difference. It didn't bother me that I had no money and very few belongings.

One week before the telephone call, everything I owned was stolen in Windhoek, Namibia. So a couple of backpackers and I hatched a brilliant plan to take tourists into the desert for sightseeing tours. On one particular tour the rear universal joints on the tail shaft of our Toyota Land Cruiser Ute snapped. We were stuck in the desert for hours until the problem was fixed.

This was not unlike the time I was stuck in the Botswana desert. I was driving the same Toyota Land Cruiser Ute and drove into a ditch. I couldn't see the track because the reflection of the sand impaired my vision. I was blinded by the glare. The impact of the crash dislodged the engine from its mounts. As a result the whole engine shifted forward into the radiator. Water spewed everywhere. We tried to patch the radiator with sealer without any luck. We used all but a few litres of water trying to fix the problem. Three days passed. It was so hot. There was no shelter from the sun. The only shade was the shadow beneath the car. We had little food or water. Not one car came by during the whole time. By the fourth day, we were wondering as to who should go for a walk. Then out of nowhere a team of Korean surveyors arrived. They were contracted to build a road through the desert. A few kilometres down the way, they were sealing the surface. So we used road tar to patch the radiator. It seemed to work for the moment but we were indifferent. I had a plane to catch.

My flight on Bulgarian airlines had already boarded when we arrived at Harare International Airport. Pushing pass the ground staff, running towards the gate, I only just made it on to the plane. Sinking into my seat, trying desperately to get comfortable, I sat quietly thinking about the last few days. Suddenly, my thoughts were interrupted by yelling, pushing—some sort of commotion. I heard my name. I sank deeper into my seat. The furore came closer. Security guards were trying to contain the commotion. Men were pushing and shoving in the aisle, bumping into passengers, and spilling their drinks. To my surprise, one of men was my German backpacker friend. I was extremely attracted to him during our time together, travelling through Namibia and Botswana. By the expression on his face, I honestly thought this was a scene from *An Officer and a Gentleman*. He looked like he was about to confess his undying love for me. Everyone on the plane was cheering and encouraging the scene to unfold. He stood before me, exhausted by his efforts to get past security, and said, "Mish, you have the keys to the truck!"

I arrived at Heathrow Airport in November, wearing a pair of 501 jeans that I tore into shorts and a white T-shirt. My luggage consisted of a brown bag that I bought in Namibia to hold chess pieces that I'd purchased in Malawi. That was it. As soon as I stepped outside, reality hit. It was freezing. I rang my Dad, charges reversed, and asked if he could wire $100 into my account. With the money, I intended to buy a coat from the thrift shop. I had no money to book accommodation, no clothes to wear, and nowhere to go, so I decided to go to a pub to get warm. I grabbed a table near the fire and decided to visit the bathroom to wash my face, tidy my hair, and remove some of the desert dust off my clothes. I must have been in there for some time, as security came storming in and dragged me out of the bathroom. That was two bouts with security within twenty-four hours.

They took me to my table and asked me to show them the contents of my brown bag. You must remember back in the early nineties, were there was a lot of unrest in England due to the IRA bombings.

I must have looked very suspicious dressed in ripped jeans and a T-shirt, plus I left my brown bag unattended at the table, which wasn't very clever. When the contents of my bag were noted and when I had the chance to explain my sad story about being detained in Katio Melino and having everything stolen, including my camera and film in Windhoek, my brief African romance with my German backpacker friend, the car key episode, and arriving in London with only hand-carved chess pieces to fly home to Australia for a wedding, the whole pub laughed. I was treated to drinks the entire evening. By closing time I wasn't feeling the cold.

The Long Way Home

I may have told a lie when I said there were no flights from London to Australia, except via Los Angeles, Tahiti, and then Sydney. Since Mum was financing my flight, I thought it was an opportune time to lose weight. I had become a bit chunky whilst travelling, especially pounding on the pounds in London. My intention was to fly to a remote Tahitian island and spend a week swimming, tanning, and eating prunes. By the time I flew home I had achieved my goal. That said, I will probably avoid prunes for the remainder of my life. My first port of call was to visit my Dad, but I was desperate to see my first love in the hope our relationship would pick up where it left off. To be honest, I wasn't sure where the relationship stood. Nonetheless, I was keen, so we agreed to meet at our favourite pub in Balmain. I spent the afternoon finding the right dress, hat (what's that?), and getting ready. I was so excited. I borrowed my Dad's car and drove to The Exchange Hotel in Balmain.

Our eyes met the moment I walked in. I felt the same feeling as I did twelve years ago. I knew he was the one. All of his mates were there too! Strange? I asked what was going on. Somehow I'd managed to fly home on the day of his bachelor party, and the wedding I was invited to was his! Bad timing? That ended the twelve-year stint pretty abruptly.

On reflection, I was pretty upset about the news of his wedding, and it brought to the surface the attraction I felt towards him. From the very moment I was introduced, it was strong. It felt like I had always known him. In fact, we were married in a past life (the one where I was Amish), but it was not a successful marriage. In that life he was obsessive to the point of abusive. There was evidence of the same behaviour in this life, but I was too naïve to notice. Many times he would follow me, without my knowing, to confirm I was where I said I would be. He was so suspicious of my every move. After I was fired from the pub in the Rocks, I secured employment at the Regent of Sydney. I worked in the club bar as a cocktail waitress. My shift finished after midnight most nights and generally security would walk you back to your car. This particular night the weather was horrid, windy, cold and pouring with rain. I decided to run back to my car without the security escort. I approached my car from the passenger side, and to my greatest surprise a man jumped out from behind the driver's seat and grabbed me. I managed to pull free and ran screaming back to the hotel. Fortunately I was not hurt or harmed in any way. In the days that followed, I spent many hours at the police station, looking through folders and folders of photos trying to identify my attacker. There was serious concern for my well-being as two girls were recently murdered in the same area and their bodies were dumped under the Harbour Bridge. Apparently, I was similar in appearance and could have been the next victim. The police were hoping I could identify the killer. I will never forget his eyes. It wasn't the killer. In the end the police thought it was a homeless man looking for refuge from the awful weather.

Matters of the Heart

When it comes to matters of the heart, the heart is the core of emotions, passion, love, and deep affection. It is a place of compassion, care, concern, friendliness, kindness, charity, and goodwill. Acts of altruism, unselfishness, philanthropy, and benevolence are shown here. In more than many ways the heart is a metaphor for an individual's innermost core or spiritual centre. It may take many lifetimes to reach this point or many lifetime experiences, where reaction and response has determined the awaking of this energy centre. It is said that when you reach anahata chakra you have become a yogi. Before then, you are a yogi practitioner.

However, there is an important point to note. For some individuals, anahata can be awakened at random. If this were the case, Swami Satyananda says that you must awaken the lower chakras and their related parts of the brain. Therefore, in order to awaken the whole brain, all the chakras must be awakened.

As we move into the fifth dimension, we will experience "a shift of ages," as foreseen by the ancients. The "Age of Aquarius" has been referred to as the "time of no time." At the moment we are "stuck" in a time warp, where time is of importance. Throughout this transition, the planet and humanity will continue to experience radical changes within the vibration and corresponding consciousness, hence, moving from being "stuck" to "unstuck," awakening anahata chakra. We will enter into a new way of thinking where one will move beyond the realms of karma and what it dictates.

Swami Satyananda believes the awakening of anahata and all the chakras is an important event in human evolution. He states it should not be confused with mysticism or occultism, as the awakening of the chakras will have significant relevance to our state of mind and consciousness. In the text Kundalini Tantra, he articulates that in this current state of mind or dimension, individuals are not capable of handling the affairs of life. Love and hatred and our current relationships with people reflect the quality of our thinking. He describes the suffering and agony we face and frustrations that are felt are not so much the circumstance of life but more to the responses of the mind. He is not alone in this belief. The spiritual community on a global basis is also unified in the idea that everything in existence is about to evolve and this evolution will have a significant effect in our mind and body.

CHAPTER 5

Vishuddhi

Speaking your Truth

Vishuddhi is the chakra of communication and diplomacy. It is connected to speaking your truth and honesty without feelings of guilt or remorse. The tendency to control others or to feel dominated by others or the feelings of superiority or inferiority are removed when this chakra is nourished by the practice of yoga.

I have been riddled with guilt for most of my life. I have felt guilty for having too much fun, for not working hard enough, for working too hard, and for not having enough fun. Guilty for the sake of guilt, which indecently serves no purpose and has damaging effects on your health and well-being.

One of the qualities needed for spiritual growth is the practice of detachment. This is evident when we arrive at vishuddhi. To practice detachment doesn't suggest abandoning life and becoming reclusive from the modern world. Rather, it is to maintain a sense of perspective when faced with overwhelming situations. I know this to be true. Every time I am confronted with a problem, where there appears no possible solution, I am reminded of the teachings of the Dali Lama. I share the problem with a power higher than myself and genuinely remove myself from the emotions that are entwined, which are more than likely to be guilt and fear. To keep a distance from my own involvement and thoughts, to be unaffected either way by the outcome seems to serve a better purpose. To become more of an observer to my life and impartial to events appears to be a healthier solution.

This notion brings to mind a famous quote by Shakespeare in *King Lear*. "When we are born, we cry that we are come to this great stage of fools." Uttered by King Lear in his darkest moment sheds light into the disappointment he feels. Probably not the best example for detachment, but it does explain the concept that events are sometimes outside our control. Taken from Act 3, scene 7, the following quote is more appropriate:

> "All the world's a stage, and all the men and women
> merely players;
> They have their exits and their entrances,
> And one man in his time plays many parts…"

The quote speaks clearly about our role in life and the seven stages of the life cycle. In essence, life will continually present situations and events that are out of our control. To become detached and to remove personal involvement helps redirect energy to higher purposes for spiritual growth and development. What is important is to stay vigilant and honest and to always speak your truth, whilst practising diplomacy.

CHAPTER 6

Ajna Chakra

The Meeting of Great Minds

The yogic journey is never purely physical. The practice of asanas will definitely tone and strengthen the muscles, increase flexibility, improve circulation, nurture the nervous system, nourish the organs, and balance the systems of the body. Slow, rhythmic, and deep breathing will enhance the faculties of the brain by inducing content states of mind. In fact, the practise of pranayama establishes regular breathing patterns, which in turn establishes a healthy body and the removal of energy blockages. Through the practice of the shatkarmas the body can remove toxins, balance pH levels, and purify the blood. The shatkarmas are also used to balance the three doshas in the body: kapha with mucus, pitta with bile, and vata with wind. According to both hatha and Ayurveda, an imbalance of the doshas can result in illness. Therefore, it is essential to undertake a regular practice of yoga postures and pranayama, combined with the cleansing and purification of the shatkarmas, to prepare the body for the successful progression along the spiritual path.

However, the journey along the spiritual path can be erratic, sometimes inconsistent and turbulent. When each of the chakras is awakened there contains within a store or memory of the karmas and samskaras, which may be pleasant, unpleasant, positive, negative, good, and bad. The awakening of any chakra will bring forward a surge of feelings and emotions that the individual may or may not be prepared to deal with at the time. In many yogic texts it is advised to purify the mind as well to best equip the individual with the necessary skills to understand the process. The purification of the mind begins at ajna chakra, where three main energies, ida, pingala, and sushumna, meet as one "third-eye chakra."

The three main energies are part of a huge network of energy circuits called nadis. In Sanskrit, the word *nadi* means "movement." In the sacred book Rigveda, nadi means, "stream." Therefore, nadis are pathways in the body that move energy along a network of channels. Unlike muscles, ligaments, tendons, or organs a nadi cannot be seen under an X-ray. If a doctor were to surgically open a human body, a nadi cannot be seen. However, they do exist in the subtle body and follow similar pathways to the nervous system.

The Nadis

Ayurveda mentions seventy-two thousand different nadis, whereas tantra identifies fourteen principal nadis, of which the following are the three most important:

1. Ida is the energy within the personality, which is passive, receptive, feminine, and negative. On a physical level it is cold, representing the moon and is associated with the

River Ganga (Ganges). On the mental plane, it relates to the emotions and intuition. Ida originates at mooladhara, passing each and every chakra to arrive on the left side of ajna.

2. Pingala can be defined as dynamic, active, and masculine, possessing the positive aspect of the personality. It is red hot, representing the solar energy, and is associated with the River Yamuna. Also originating at mooladhara, pingala arrives on the right side of ajna.

3. Sushumna is the central channel and is associated with the River Saraswati. Sushumna passes through the spinal column, starting at Mooladhara and completing the journey at sahasra chakra. Sahasra chakra generally remains dormant when the other nadis flow and is activated only when the breath simultaneously comes through both nostrils. It can be activated by pranayama and kundalini practices. Though ida and pingala have contrasting functions, they are complementary and must be balanced for total health, well-being, and peace of mind.

Any imbalance to the subtle flow of energy can have detrimental effects on personality as well as general health. For instance, if the right side, or pingala, is dominant, the personality becomes dry and aggressive, and the ego becomes strong and forceful. As a result, sensitivity to emotions is lost. If not dealt with, this right-sided behaviour can lead to health concerns including heart disease. If ida energy is weakened by the demands of pingala, joy, happiness, and intuition are comprised.

Yogis have documented the connection between the breath and its influence on the functioning of the brain over the years. In meditative experience they could feel the flow of energy in the nerves moving into and out of the mind and body. Using methods or techniques, they found ways to control the flow to develop greater sensitivity and strength. Shambhavi mudra and trataka are two very powerful techniques used to awaken Ajna Chakra by balancing ida and pingala nadis. Likewise, nadi shodhana pranayama is a useful practice to balance the subtle flow of energy.

Nadi Shodhana

Nadi shodhana, or the alternate nostril breathing, is suitable for beginning and advanced students. Nadi means channel and refers to the energy pathways through which prana flows. Shodhana means cleansing, so nadi shodhana means channel cleaning.

Benefits

Nadi shodhana calms the mind, soothes anxiety and stress, balances the left and right hemispheres of the brain, and promotes clear thinking.

How to do it

- Hold your right hand up and place your middle fingers between your eyes and the thumb next to your right nostril. Close the right nostril by pressing gently against it with your thumb, and inhale through the left nostril. The breath should be slow, steady, and full.

- Now close the left nostril by pressing gently against it with your ring finger and pinkie, and open your right nostril by relaxing your thumb and exhale fully with a slow and steady breath.
- Inhale through the right nostril, close it, and then exhale through the left nostril.

That's one complete round of nadi shodhana. To sum up:

- Inhale through the left
- Exhale through the right
- Inhale through the right nostril
- Exhale through the left

Begin with five to ten rounds and add more as you feel ready. Remember to keep your breathing slow, easy and full. Nadi Shodhana helps control stress and anxiety. It also helps soothe the adrenal glands and calm the nervous system.

Ajna Chakra

In Sanskrit, *ajna* means, "to perceive," "to know," and "to command." Our physical eyes are the tools with which we see tangibles, whereas the "third eye" above and below the eyebrows offers the ability to perceive the intangible, things for which there is no concrete evidence. Interestingly, the symbol for this chakra is a two-petal lotus, with a circle in between containing an inverted triangle. Within the triangle is the symbol for OM. The petals are like two eyes, with the centre circle representing the third eye. This is further likened to the side hemispheres of the brain working in harmony.

"Hat Trick": the Significance of Three

Along the yogic path, we have discussed the practice of asanas to prepare the body. In the eight limbs of raja yoga, asanas are third on the list. In chapter 1 we discussed the healing properties of Ayurveda, where it is suggested to balance the three doshas to prevent illness. The convergence of the three main nadis in the body meet at ajna, just like in Hindu mythology where the three great rivers converge into one. The Ganga (ida), Jamuna (pingala), and Saraswati (which represents sushumna) converge at Allahabad. The relevance of asanas, Ayurveda, and ajna can be seen here as we draw significance upon each of the meanings. These three components are essential for the purification of the mind. It is said that when the mind is pure and focused, and the three main nadis meet at ajna, a shift in consciousness takes place.

However, the mind is a difficult piece of apparatus to control. Thoughts are constantly bombarding the mind every second of the day. Even in concentration, distractions can occur. So how do you purify the mind?

It is here we turn to Patanjali, a yogi and author of historic yoga texts to answer the question, "How does one bring stillness and clarity to a busy mind?"

Patanjali wrote the Yoga Sutras, which essentially have to do with the mind and its modifications. The sutras deal with training the mind to achieve oneness with the universe. The aim of yoga is to set the mind free from the restrictions of matter. The mind being the highest form of matter needs to be freed from the vrittis (meaning "whirlpool"; it indicates the contents of mental awareness are disturbances in the medium of consciousness) to become pure. This is made obvious by Patanjali's definition of yoga: "Yoga is the cessation of the mind." As such, yoga is the state of no mind, when the activity of thinking ceases to exist and all thoughts have disappeared. Every aspirant of Patanjali's sutras are able to refine aspiration, clarify thoughts, and essentially strengthen and sharpen their focus on spiritual self-discipline by accommodating various techniques of mind control, visualisation, pranayama, and asana practice. It is here that Patanjali skilfully and tactfully integrates a system of yoga that moves from one sutra to the next with such precision and faultless logic.

According to Patanjali, if the question, "What is yoga?" were asked, the reply would be, "Yoga is a way to rule or govern the subtle nature of human personality." To continue along this line of thought, if asked, "What is the result of this ability to govern?" the answer would be, "Yogash chitta vritti nirodhah." In these famous words, Patanjali stipulates that yoga is the restraint of the modifications of the mind. He states the essential meaning of yoga without any objection or argument, is the process of purification. He acknowledged that from the outset, more consideration is given to practical instruction than theoretical knowledge in yoga. It was understood, therefore, that the yoga student of sutras already had some prior understanding of yoga and was prepared to undergo a demanding daily discipline. As Swami Niranjan states, "The second and third sutras are only states of attainment after you have begun the practice of yoga."

After you have started the practice of yoga, you can control the mental modifications. In yogash chitta vritti nirodhah, there is reference to chitta, vritti, and nirodhah. The mind of chitta is said to operate on many levels, as it is responsible for our thoughts, feelings, intentions, motives, and desires, which are naturally inclined to egoism. From egoism evolves prejudice and judgment, which provide the basis for pleasure and pain. This creates anxiety, stress, and depression. Patanjali discusses the root cause of suffering in the final chapter, "Samadhi Pada."

However, according to Patanjali, the true nature of chitta (the mind) is when it is not modified by external influences and their internal impressions. For as long as modifications persist, the mind unwittingly identifies with them, falling into passivity, habitude, and pain.

Patanjali describes these afflictions as the vrittis. There are five types of vrittis. The first is known as pramana—direct knowledge, the second viparyaya—wrong knowledge, vikalpa—fancy, nidra—sleep, and smriti—memory. According to Patanjali, these five modifications are seen as an opportunity to observe and accept ourselves, to enable us to enquire into the depth of our personality. However, as Swami Niranjan summarises in his commentary on the sutras: "Mental modifications dissipate our energies and thoughts and prevent us from living according to the natural laws of nature. Their root causes need to be grasped controlled and transcended, if they are to be firmly removed."

According to the Bhagavad Gita, vairagya (non-attachment) is one way to stop the flow of vrittis. Non-attachment is the instrument that will cut through the bondage of maya (illusion) through the bondage of pleasure and pain. Non-attachment is important, according to Swami Niranjan, when considering self-acceptance and self-purification, for they both lead to an understanding and realisation of our inner personality.

As consciousness has circular patterns with no end or beginning, Patanjali recognises the need to stop or block the flow of movement. It is here that the meaning of Nirodhah becomes clear, as its root meaning is the "act of blocking." Therefore, nirodhah stops the fluctuations of the mind. To return to the initial question "What is yoga?" this sutra replies, "Yoga is the blocking of the patterns arising in all the dimensions of consciousness." What appears to be a rhetorical question is in fact the beginning of an ordered sequence in the evolution of yoga.

On initial investigation, I understood yoga to be derived from the Sanskrit word *yui*, which means "to join or yoke." It was my understanding that yoga was the union of mind and body by the integration of asana and pranayama. That was my depth of understanding. Now when I consider the position of this sutra in the full sequence, I realise my initial interpretation was superficial, hence limited to my knowledge and understanding. It was my aim, therefore, to study the true essence of "What is yoga?" to further my experience and education and to become more familiar and intimate with Patanjali's Yoga Sutras.

So I decided to study sutra 1:24, Ishvara Pranidhana. The translation of Ishvara Pranidhana in its simplest form is a combination of two concepts. ishvara, when translated, means God, Lord, Supreme Being, or Life Force, whereas pranidhana means attention to, to love, surrender, have faith, and unite. A comforting way to interpret Ishvara Pranidhana is to have "attentiveness to God" or "to surrender to a higher source." In other words, surrendering to the practice of yoga.

It is interesting to note that whilst Patanjali is an advocate for Samkhya philosophy, he makes no reference to God throughout the sutras except for this one word, Ishvara. In the Samkhya system, the principle thought is that reality has two aspects: Nashwara and Ishvara. Nashwara is the decaying principle relating to the manifest dimension of existence, whereas Ishvara is the non-decaying principle relating to the unmanifest. So Ishvara is the final term, going beyond the realm of appearance, beyond the experience of name, form, and idea.

Out of the many traditions of yoga, there appears to be a common goal of attainment. "Inner individual harmony," Swami Niranjan states, "with the universal cosmic consciousness" this is the position of preference. Swami Niranjan further elaborates: "The aim is always one but over a period of time the practitioners who came to an understanding of the individual's relationship with the cosmic consciousness realised we all function at different levels of existence, evolution and consciousness. The manifestation of energy is different in each one of us" (Swami Niranjan, *Yoga Sadhana Panorama* 1997).

Therefore, it can be stated that a different yoga is required for different people. An individual has their right to express freedom of choice. This is evident in the millions of gods and goddesses worshipped in India. Traditionally, many monks in India have revered Shiva as the archetypal yogi, whereas others are drawn to Vishnu, especially in the incarnations of Rama or Krishna. There are the feminine manifestations of divinity like Lakshmi, Kali, or Durga. In fact, there is nothing stated in the basic philosophical structure of the sutras about one form of divinity. Patanjali carefully refers to the word *va*, which means "or," hence Ish "va" ra. The meaning of pranidhana is to use your own personal approach to reach the divine. So you can choose and connect with whomever best suits your needs or beliefs. This may be Jesus, Buddha, Mohammad, Krishna, or none of these. Rather than be indoctrinated by one particular dogma, Patanjali is more like an athletic coach guiding you to make choices along the path of Samadhi (a non-dualistic state where one becomes one with the universe).

There is, however, the concept of Ishvara Pranidhana. As a term, it means to surrender to the unmanifest reality, which has the possibility of taking any form but which in itself has no name, form, or attitude in the Yoga Sutras. The great Yogi Sri Krishnamacharya reinforced this concept in his teaching. Possibly one of the most influential personalities in the spread of yoga to the world, Sri Krishnamacharya taught his students to use their own language, imagery, names, beliefs, and mores to deepen their understanding and further their connection to Ishvara Pranidhana.

Surrender, Surrender, Surrender

The concepts of surrender, individual faith, and commitment to a higher reality than the self may be a weird concept to many, as to "let go" is a massive step when confronted with financial problems, unemployment, sickness, heartache, and loss. In times of hardship, we tend to cling more desperately to the idea that money, career, and status give us our identity. Holding on to routine, habit, possessions, and materialism, we try to control the uncontrollable.

Ishvara Pranidhana suggests the opposite. It implies complete trust and willingness to open your heart and be in the moment. In the words of Ramakrishna, "Surrender is like falling from a tree without flinching a muscle," further implying to "let go'" to any preconceived notion or idea of "what it should be" and to just "let it be." Paul McCarthy and John Lennon said it in their famous song and so did Swami Niranjan when he said "Hari Om Tat Sat" at the conclusion of his visit to Australia.

For Patanjali, Ishvara Pranidhana is to open your heart to a higher reality other than yourself. It is a way or means of dissolving the constant fluctuations of the mind in an attempt to reach samadhi, the unified state of yoga. This element is an essential key to yoga. Why is it essential? It's essential because Ishvara shifts the focus from the "self" from individual concern and perception that causes much pain and distraction, but mostly separation from the higher source. Since Ishvara Pranidhana focuses on complete surrender of one's ego to unite with a greater power, its essence then is to dissolve the concept of the ego and move towards unification with the universe. Here the concept of duality is destroyed and dissolved.

"What is duality?" you may ask. Duality is the ego and the ego is the constant reminder of the self. As long as you remember yourself, you cannot forget yourself. With the memory of the self, you cannot become one with the universe. Therefore, when the ego dissolves and the individual becomes one with a higher reality, there is no more duality. How do we do this?

In the Yoga Sutras, Patanjali repeatedly highlights Ishvara Pranidhana as one of the five niyames, or inner practices. Let's pause here for a moment to discuss the yamas and niyamas. Within the Yoga Sutras, Patanjali gave equal importance to the yamas and niyamas within the eight-limbed yoga system. Many practitioners jump straight onto their yoga mat and start bending and twisting into asanas (poses). However, the second limb, niyamas, contain five essential internal practices, which extend from the ethical codes of conduct provided in the first limb. Niyamas provide a basis for a yogi's internal environment of mind, body and spirit. To incorporate niyamas into daily practice helps provide a positive environment in which self-discipline and inner strength are required for progress along the yogic path.

Within the niyamas are five parts. The first, shaucha, is purification. This extends beyond asana, pranayama, and meditation. It involves positive thoughts and foods. It includes socializing with positive, happy people and undertaking healthy activities. The essential message here is to eat healthy and nutritious foods, drink plenty of water, and avoid drugs, alcohol, cigarettes, sugar, and saturated fats. It is best to avoid negative emotions like anger, jealousy, and hatred or at least find a healthy way to express them for healing to take place.

The next niyama is contentment, santosha. This is a toughie for some. For reassurance, take comfort in the wisdom of Mother Teresa, who said, "Be happy in the moment, that's enough. Each moment is all we need, not more." Great yogis tell us that when we are perfectly content with what life gives us, we feel true joy and happiness. The mind can be easily distracted into thinking that material possessions, wealth, and success can bring happiness. However, these feelings are usually temporary. Practising santosha frees the mind from delusion and unnecessary suffering of wanting things to be different. Instead it fills the soul with gratitude and joy for all of life's blessings.

Having to do something that you don't really want to is the key issue of tapas, the third niyama. I can completely relate to this one. At the ashram, I really struggled with karma yoga, especially when the chore didn't make sense to me. During my years of study, I have carried rocks to the top of a mountain, made a road with the same rocks, weeded and planted gardens, painted buildings, painted T-shirts, cleaned toilets, cleaned rooms—the list goes on.

After years of karma yoga, emphasis on the word karma, I finally understood its meaning. I recall the time our house was on the market and everyone at home was busy cleaning and preparing for the sale. I rang my husband and asked what he was doing, to which his reply was cleaning the screens. I was pretty pleased to be at the ashram avoiding boring but necessary jobs. After lunch, on the same day, I asked the swami in charge of kitchen duties, was there any other chore. I didn't expect a reply. To my surprise he said, "Yes, you can clean the screens!"

Like tapas, karma yoga is doing something you don't want to do, but in the big picture, it will have a positive effect in your life. How does it work? A fire or heat is produced when our will conflicts with a desire. This fire burns up mental and physical impurities, which transforms laziness and selfishness into motivation and kindness. Therefore, tapas can heighten one's experience of spirituality by the purification of unconscious impulses and poor behaviour to build willpower and personal strength. Through my experience with karma yoga, I struggle less when doing things I don't enjoy. Rather, I see the task at hand as an opportunity to do something that is bigger than my own needs and personal satisfaction. To perform a task for the greater benefit of others and not just myself certainly makes cleaning screens easier. This leads beautifully to svadhyaya, the fourth niyama.

Svadhyaya is the ability to learn from life's lessons. Self-study allows the opportunity to see our flaws and weaknesses, to examine our actions and responses to everyday situations. It is from this awareness we grow and learn and become the best person we can be. OM namah shivaya!

Ishvara Pranidhana is the last of the niyamas. *Surrender, surrender, and surrender!* In summary, the fifth niyama is the complete surrender to a higher source. This niyama fuses two concepts together, the devotion to something greater than the self and karma yoga. To do this, our actions must be altruistic and seen as an offering to something greater than ourselves. This could be as simple as a hand gesture (mudra) in your yoga practice or salute to the sun (worshipping the sun), or chanting the Gayatri mantra, Maha Mrityunjaya or the Durgas.

A beautiful example of Ishvara Pranidhana is the way the Balinese light incense and offer flowers and fruit to the gods at the beginning of each day. I witness this every year when I go to Bali to teach yoga. When teaching English in Thailand, I happened to be a part of Teacher's Day celebrations, whereby the students set a day aside from study to worship their teachers. We were showered with gifts ranging from flowers, fruit, breads, incense, beads, cloths, and fabrics. We were entertained by cultural performances and dance. For eight hours we sat on a stage to view the proceedings whilst monks sat by our feet and prayed. What an amazing example of giving back and showing respect to the teachers. How lucky I was to be a witness of Ishvara Pranidhana shown by the acts of dedication, devotion, and surrender.

I am neither christened nor baptised. My parents decided I should research and discover my own faith and spiritual beliefs. As a child I attended Sunday school. One year was spent at the Salvation Army, the next at the Church of England. Then there was the gap year, were I spent my collection money on lollies and sat in the park to feed the ducks every Sunday. Due to my spirited personality and adventurous nature, I was sent to a Catholic ladies college to complete my education. I even chose to study theology at university, to broaden my knowledge and understanding of religion and spirituality.

But it was yogic philosophy that caught my attention, particularly Patanjali's sutras. I believe everyone needs something to believe in and that belief should be respected. I believe in yoga. I believe yoga has the ability to not only strengthen the physical body but also improve flexibility. It has the ability to improve the functioning of the respiratory, circulatory, digestive, and hormonal systems. I tend to be a nervous person, constantly suffering from shingles, so I am attracted to asanas that calm and settle the nervous system. Yoga for me brings emotional stability and clarity of mind, which has helped with conflicting impulses and thoughts that I have experienced over the last ten years.

During this time, I have been extremely active, teaching fifteen classes a week, an owner of a healing shop, editor of a magazine, plus I have Mummy duties that are fun yet demanding. I have been mentally exhausted and at the same time over-stimulated. Further complicated by sleep deprivation, my thoughts have been scattered, disturbing, and very distracting from time to time. To reduce the element of rajas (yogic term for excitement, passion, and assertiveness), I have engaged in physical work, probably more housework than necessary, and practiced ashtanga yoga, which is a sequence of yoga postures designed by Sri K. Pattabhi Jois of India. It is a dynamic style of yoga that takes into consideration alignment, movement, and breath of asanas. The practices of bhakti yoga and ajapa japa would be beneficial for someone influenced by rajas, like myself. Likewise forward bends and inversions. In short, I could see the benefits of yoga on a daily basis. I honestly believe I survived three children under the age of two, home renovations, my husband starting a new career, two spinal surgeries, a cerebral spinal fluid puncture, a broken wrist, and the loss of my Dad because of my devotion to yoga. I believe a level of commitment is required, plus constant practice, so that in time it becomes part of your personality and individual nature. To find something in life that resonates with your higher purpose and attainment of a spiritual life, in my opinion, is a modest attempt to believe in something higher than yourself.

A Great Spiritual Coach

In his wisdom, Patanjali must have acknowledged that only a few highly developed adept individuals who studied the sutras were able to develop their knowledge and understanding of the complexities of spiritual attainment. A great rishi and fully evolved soul, Patanjali had the ability to empathize with the joys and sorrows of ordinary people. He was able to share his fruits of wisdom with those who were ready to receive it, and to those who were willing to try. His aim was to direct and guide each individual to reach his or her full potential. Therefore, he designed a system for going from the state of knowledge to the state of experience. His written presentation of a very practical system of yoga is said to be so succinct, precise, and complete that it is still a reliable guideline for those who practice yoga today.

Patanjali's Words of Wisdom

There are many different ways to approach spiritual enlightenment and for many it is overwhelming and confusing. Patanjali, in his wisdom acknowledged this and as such provided support in the form of a mantra.

The mantra is AUM (OM). As discussed earlier, ishvara is the ultimate point of supreme consciousness and it has no form. The eyes or ears cannot perceive ishvara, but through the expression of AUM it is possible to experience him or her. Therefore, AUM is the word that denotes ishvara.

Patanjali recommends that repetition (japa) of AUM needs to be used in conjunction with concentration (dhyana) for meditation to be complete. One AUM alone is not as effective. He states the contemplation of the meaning of AUM is also equally important. The meaning of A is understood in relation to the world of senses, physical body, and objective enjoyment or vishra purusha. The letter U is to be understood in relation to the subconscious mind, subjective enjoyment, or the tegas state of purusha. M to be understood in relation to the unconscious, mindlessness, no enjoyment, or prajna state of purusha. When each individual letter comes together to form the mantra AUM, all three states of consciousness are reached. However, the fourth state, turiya, is the unmanifested, unheard, and unexpressed state of purusha that transcends all other states. As ishvara has no form and is consequently difficult to reach, the word AUM is an expression that denotes ishvara. In sutra 1:28, Patanjali suggests AUM when repeated is a vehicle to reach higher states of reality.

AUM became popularised by Swami Satchitananda at Woodstock in the sixties. The festival was regarded as a pivotal point in contemporary musical history. At the same time the opening speech by Swami Satchitananda vibrated volumes around the world. It was probably here that I became familiar with the expression. When I first started teaching yoga, it was suggested not to AUM in class as this may intimidate newcomers. Now it has become accepted as a part of the practice. Students enjoy the discipline and routine of starting and completing a class with the mantra. They understand AUM is a vehicle to reach higher states of reality but also the mantra has beneficial effects on calming the nervous system. In a research project conducted in Barcelona from 1978–79, patients were asked to chant the mantra AUM five minutes before surgery. Each patient was monitored scientifically. The results indicated that the mantra had beneficial effects on heart rate and skin resistance as well as on the nervous system. As Swami Niranjan concludes, benefits that have been recognised by yogis for centuries have become evident to man today.

At this point of the journey the concept of surrender, non-duality and purification have been discussed. When we arrive at Ajna Chakra, Patanjali wrote explicitly about those whose progress is rapid and those whose efforts are mild or moderate. The level at which one achieves is subjective, but according to Patajani, as long as people believe in the method and are sincere in their intentions, they will receive the rewards from their effort.

Shiva and Shakti

Amongst the attributes of the chakras, there are two important figures that must be given consideration. They come from the Mahashivatri and it is the story of Shiva and Shakti. Shiva is the representation of consciousness, the embodiment of awareness, and the essence of masculinity, presence, purpose, and skilful means. He represents transcendence, detachment, bliss, and the path to liberation. Whereas Shakti is energy, the essence of feminine beauty, offering qualities such as nourishment, warmth, and security whilst providing change and movement.

The legend begins when Shiva and Shakti were returning from Agastya's ashram. The evening was spent listening to the story of Ram. Lord Shiva found a very distraught Lord Rama in the forest. Apparently, Ravana had kidnapped Lord Rama's wife. Unbeknownst to Shakti, Lord Rama was the incarnation of Lord Vishnu. This information was available to Shiva, and he treated Lord Rama with great respect. In Shakti's opinion, Lord Shiva gave a mere mortal too much time and energy. Displeased with Shakti's response to the kidnapping, Lord Shiva informed his wife that she should research the matter further before casting aspersions.

Using her power to change forms, Shakti was soon to learn that Lord Rama was the incarnation of Vishnu. Reporting the news to Shiva, she was surprised by his reaction. Rather than make amends and reconcile their relationship, Shiva decided to terminate their union. Shakti riddled with profound sadness, sought advice from her father, Daksha. Daksha ignored her pleas for help. Shattered and broken by her father's total disregard for her marriage and by Shiva's detachment, Shakti jumped into the Yagna Fire and immolated herself.

Lord Shiva, stricken with grief about Shakti's immolation, began to perform Rudra Tandava, the dance of destruction, and wiped out the kingdom of Daksha. Frightened by Shiva's ability to destroy the entire universe, Vishnu decided to sever Shakti's body into twelve parts, which were scattered around the planet. Where each piece fell emerged Shakti Peethas (places of worship).

Retiring to the Himalayas and undertaking a self-imposed penance, Lord Shiva spent his time in meditation. Fearful Shiva's reclusiveness would lead to asceticism, Shakti decided to reincarnate as Parvati. Initially, Lord Shiva ignored Parvati's attempts to seduce him. As such she sought the assistance of Kamadeva, the god of love and passion, who persuaded Parvati to dance in front of Shiva. Still without success, she employed other devas to win Shiva's attention.

Let's Dance

The relationship between Shiva and Shakti is the dance of consciousness and energy. Together in union, Shiva and Shakti merge and create the universe and all its manifestations. Within each and every one of us is this blend of masculine and feminine qualities that work together to create movement and change, abundance and security with presence and purpose. Energy alone cannot produce anything hence requiring consciousness to impart form. Likewise, consciousness is lost without direction and energy.

Shakti resides in mooladhara and Shiva in sahasrara chakra. When the two unite, passing each and every chakra in their path, the qualities of each chakra are displayed along the way. In union, they represent the combination of nature and divine consciousness. As such, there are no polarities here, no conflicts, and no dualities. Only everlasting joy and happiness exist, embracing compassion and total understanding. This, however, is not a destination or a conclusion, but a new beginning for new experiences and infinite possibilities.

This leads beautifully to the chakra sahasrara. However, Swami Satyananda says sahasrara is not a chakra, as often thought. He says, "Chakras are within the realm of the psyche. Consciousness manifests at different levels according to the chakra that is predominately active. Sahasrara acts through nothing … it acts through everything. Sahasrara is beyond the beyond and yet it is right here."

The Sanskrit interpretation of *sahasrara* is one thousand, and its symbology is a lotus. Together they are synonymous with infinity, but Swami Satyananda states that even the number one thousand has limitations. In his opinion, Sahasrara implies infinity, and that its magnitude and significance is vast—in fact limitless. Therefore, according to Swami Satyananda, a lotus with an infinite number of petals would best represent sahasrara.

Sahasrara then is everything and nothing. When Shiva and Shakti unite, nothing remains. Shakti is no longer Shakti, likewise Shiva is no longer Shiva. They are no longer two individual identities. They fuse into one. Many traditions, religions, and philosophies have described this experience in their own way. Some call it nirvana, others kundalini, samadhi, self-realisation, enlightenment, communion, and so forth.

In the ultimate union, there is no "I" or "you" or "they"; rather the experience, the experiencer, and the experienced are the same. At such a level, intellect makes way for experience and knowledge. At sahasrara, the possibility of space and time is boundless. There are no restrictions set by previous patterns and convention. No wonder seers and sages have described this experience as bliss.

CHAPTER 7

Bhagavad Gita

So How Do We Deal with Life?

As individuals, we are constantly bombarded by situations that require different responses. Conflicts are inevitable in the course of life. How do we deal with stress and pressure with equanimity of mind without comprising our values, beliefs, and principles?

One of the ancient Indian texts that offer some insight into the resolution of such a question is the Bhagavad Gita. It is one of three texts written on yoga. Comprised of eighteen chapters, the Bhagavad Gita discusses three main areas: jnana, karma, and bhakti. The purpose of the text is to outline the spiritual foundation of human existence and the fulfilment of one's responsibilities (dharma). The pursuit of spiritual freedom is not new. It has been a quest for mankind since the dawn of civilisation. One of the reasons for its extraordinary popularity in contemporary society is that the Bhagavad Gita transcends the narrow confines of religion, race, nationality, and gender. Its sheer universality is relevant to every human being in every age and every ethos.

The setting of the Bhagavad Gita is just before a great battle takes place. It is a battle of kinship, a battle of revenge, and a battle for honour. The Pandava and Kaurava forces are assembled on the battlefield. Arjuna, the Pandava, is a great and brave warrior who suddenly becomes overwhelmed with grief and confusion when he realises he has to fight his own relatives. Faced with such a moral dilemma of whether to fulfil his duty as a warrior and take responsibility for the bloodshed that is to ensue, or the action of non-action, he turns to the eternal teacher Lord Krishna for guidance. It is here that one of the greatest expeditions of life and liberation, freedom and responsibility begins. In the various solutions provided by Krishna, whether of action, knowledge, or devotion, it is clear that a relationship of trust, faith, and devotion evolves between teacher and student.

The Teacher and the Student

It is Krishna's approach to solving such a moral dilemma and his description of the ways to reach God in chapter 12 that has my interest. In particular, chapter 12, verses 5 to 12.

The way in which Krishna outlines methods to reach God seems fair and reasonable. He gives a clear and methodical approach to worship without judgment and criticism. His teachings are non threatening or forceful as the emphasis is upon acceptance of one's abilities and limitations. For not only does Krishna give people the freedom to choose their spiritual path, there is the constant reminder that it doesn't really matter what we do, as long as we do it with an inner dedication and devotion.

At the outset of chapter 12, Arjuna wants to know who is the better yogi: one who follows the path of devotion, looking upon God with form, or one who looks upon the formless and imperceptible Brahman (the highest reality). Krishna states that all devotees who worship God with faith and adore him are praiseworthy. However, of the two paths, worshipping a God without form is very difficult and troublesome. Swami Sivananda's commentary on the twelfth discourse further suggests that yoga of devotion (bhakti yoga) is much easier than the yoga of knowledge (jnana yoga). It is in 12:5 that the differences between bhakti and jnana yoga become apparent.

In pointing out the difference, it suggests worship with form begins with devotion to idols or symbols of God. As this is visible to the senses, it can be thought of by the mind, thus making worship more attainable. For those who choose to follow the impersonal way to spiritual realisation, the path is more difficult. They have to understand the unmanifest representation of the Supreme through such Vedic literature as the Upanishads, learn the language, and understand the non-perceptual feeling and have the ability to process this.

The following comment by Swami Prabhupāda appears to be an appropriate inference: "For those minds that are attached to the unmanifest, impersonal feature of the Supreme, advancement is the very troublesome. To make progress in that discipline is always difficult."

In my opinion, formless worship is harder for humans to practise. It is extremely difficult to fix the mind on the unthinkable, indefinable, and incomprehensible, as the unmanifest is beyond speech and thought, the organs of knowledge. In his commentaries, Swami Prabhupāda offers a very strong point of view. His position is that, "One should not take up this process, as there is the danger of turning to atheism. This process of focusing the attention on the unmanifest, the inconceivable, which is beyond the approach of the senses, as already expressed in this verse, should never be encouraged at any time, especially this age."

According to the Bhagavad Gita, single-minded devotion to God is the surest path to self-realisation. In whatever way a devotee approaches God, God will undoubtedly accept him or her. The Bhagavad Gita acknowledges men will approach God from all directions, but it is in their effort and dedication that makes the difference. Hence the notion that God receives all devotees is the central theme in 12:6–7, when Krishna responds to Arjuna's question, "Who is the better yogi?"

> *Those who worship me, giving up all their activities unto me without deviation, engage in devotional service and always meditating upon me, having their minds fixed upon me, O son of Prtha, they are speedily rescued from the ocean of moral existence.* (Swami Sivananda, *Bhagavad Gita* 2003, 301)

The purport of this verse is that one should fix their mind fully on Krishna in order to achieve him. In other words, one should be exclusive in their intentions and devotion to the Lord. Swami Prabhupada in his commentary on the Bhagavad Gita confirmed this when he states, "The Supreme Lord can only be appreciated by devotional service. One should work only for him. It doesn't matter in what kind of work one engages, but that work should be done only for him."

In Swami Sivananda's commentary, he adds: "One who fixes his mind on the Lord exclusively, who burns up the fruit of actions by offering them to the Lord and who thus destroys any power in the actions to bear fruit, and who has abandoned even the idea of liberation, is soon lifted by the Lord from the moral plane to the abode of immortality" (Swami Sivananda, *Bhagavad Gita* 2003, 301).

In the verses to follow, Lord Krishna offers a clear and systematic approach to reach God. In 12:9 he states, "If thou art unable to fix thy mind steadily on me, then by the yoga of constant practice do thou seek to reach me, O Arjuna."

Constant Practice

Simply put, abhyasa is constant practice. To be effective, however, abhyasa must be regularly and constantly practised over a long period of time. It is the means to control the mind and fix it to one point together with vairagya. It involves pratyahara. In Patanjali's raja yoga, Pratyahara is the fifth limb and it is the skill of withdrawing the mind from sensual forces. Control over the senses requires mastery and is a difficult task to perform. It can be achieved however, by various yoga practices including focusing on a single point in the body like nose tip gazing (Nasikagra Drishti) or by a meditation practice like antar mouna or pranayama. The practice of abhyasa is like the momentum of a rolling stone. It builds upon itself, and the more you practice pratyahara the faster you will reach your destination. It is Lord Krishna's opinion that the yoga of constant practice will offer a systematic approach to reach God. Swami Sivananda also believes the constant effort to separate or detach oneself from the illusory five sheaths or layers of human existence that range from the dense physical body to the more subtle levels of emotions, mind, and spirit and to identify oneself with the ātman (inner self) is also abhyasa.

Swami Prabhupada is an advisory of bhakti yoga as a means to reach God. He believes the regulatory practice of rising early; bathing, prayer, and practise contribute to the yoga of devotion. Furthermore, the offering to a deity the collection of flowers and preparation of cooked foodstuffs on a daily basis is a firm commitment to abhyasa. He also advises the practice of bhakti yoga should be under the guidance of a swami or guru.

In bhakti yoga, there appears certain rules and practices that one should follow with the aim or intention to purify the heart by absolute and ceremonial devotion. Whatever is offered to the Lord—a leaf, flower, fruit, or water—it is the intention that is more important than the offering itself. As long as it is done with pure and untainted devotion, its meaning and purpose is felt. This becomes more clear in 12:10, where Krishna implies that, "If one is unable to partake in the regulative practices of abhyasa yoga, even for short periods of time or at least resort to the worship of images of God, then one should try to control the senses and remember me in your actions." If you do this, he states, "Everything is an offering to God."

At some point this may be demanding for some and in his wisdom Krishna recognised the limitations of man. Therefore, in 12:11 he says that if the yoga of mediation, yoga of constant practice, and the performance of actions for the sake of the Lord are too difficult, he suggests to "abandon the fruits of all actions." What this statement means is rather than engage in devotional services, try voluntary work or national service, where your intention is to help and serve others. In congruence with this notion, Swami Prabhupada says this may lead to or develop into devotional service to the Supreme Lord, one day in the future.

To collate my thoughts at this point, there appears two ways to reach God. The first is more direct, as stated in 12:6; however, this is not possible for everyone. Therefore, Krishna suggests an indirect method in 12:9–12. It also becomes clear that Arjuna's path is more direct as he is already at the stage of devotional service to the Supreme Lord. This becomes more evident as the dialogue between Krishna and Arjuna develops throughout the verses. To reach this stage, Arjuna had to process and evaluate his situation, interpret his response, and take appropriate action. Parallels can be drawn here to all people and their reaction to everyday situations. In every situation, an appropriate response is required. This response can be easily influenced by our desires and other extraneous factors, which are irrelevant to it. At times it is difficult to approach a situation with equanimity of mind as we are constantly being bombarded with circumstances that test our values, beliefs, and principles.

Similar to Arjuna, there exists within each of us a battlefield, where the forces of nature are constant. At that moment on the battlefield, Arjuna's responsibility was to fight. Due to the perplexity of the situation, he lost sight of his responsibility (dharma) by allowing associations that were irrelevant to overwhelm him. However, due to Arjuna's ambition to move towards a state of clarity, or "sthita prajna," he chose to follow the path offered by Lord Krishna. In such a state, T. V. K. Desikachar suggests a person must destroy ignorance through the knowledge of the self and control the senses through action. In essence, the means to reach a goal or a desired outcome is to take action without attachment. Action is an inevitable aspect of life. It is impossible to live without action. As such, "to live is to act" is a continuing theme in chapter 3 of the Bhagavad Gita.

According to Indian tradition, what the action must be is determined by one's dharma. Arjuna's dharma was to fight, as he was a great and respected warrior. In this life my dharma is to be a wife, mother, and teacher. As a parent, I have the responsibility of providing for my children and ensuring their safety, well-being, and happiness. The institution of marriage implies other responsibilities. As a teacher, I have certain norms, codes of conduct, professional etiquette, and duty of care for my students. In the course of life we have different roles that entail responsibilities of varying degrees, but knowing one's dharma and following it faithfully, by avoiding distractions that lie on the path, ensure progress towards a goal. Thus the path towards spiritual freedom begins with the dedicated performance of those actions that are socially and professionally dictated by one's dharma.

The way in which Krishna guides Arjuna towards self-realisation and spiritual freedom appeals to me. For one, I am aware of my limitations without creating unreasonable expectations of myself. I am able to begin my spiritual journey, firstly by releasing attachment to the outcome of my actions. Prior to the study of the Bhagavad Gita, every action I performed had required a result, an outcome that measured my success. I am beginning to relinquish this notion by completing tasks with a different mindset. Instead of measuring my result for personal reward, I try to surrender my actions to the Lord. In doing this I have found significant changes taking place. Initially, my workload feels easier and more enjoyable. More importantly, I have started to notice less anger and resentment taking place. I tend to be less stressed and anxious. Finally, I have experienced a sense of freedom, as I am no longer bound by doubt or feel insecure by the demands and expectations that I often place on myself. I realise this is only the beginning, but it is this aspect that makes the teachings of the Bhagavad Gita so significant.

In response to the opening statement, "How does one face situations with equanimity of mind?" according to the Bhagavad Gita, the answer lies in becoming a true devotee. It is a person who is selfless, who treats likes and dislikes, happiness and misery the same, who is ever forgiving and always content, and whose commitment to God is sincere. One who is pure in intention, who renounces all fruit, whether good or bad, who is untouched by the forces of desire and has discipline, reason, and purpose in life can face situations with equanimity of mind.

In summary, the yoga of the Bhagavad Gita begins at a gross level with emphasis on performing one's duty and responsibilities without any expectations. In a gradual progression from conflict to clarity, which embraces knowledge (jnana yoga), action (karma yoga), and devotion (bhakti yoga) to reach a stage of complete surrender and total absorption.

Does Yoga Offer the Answers?

In my opinion, yes.

However, the answer is not simple. Yoga has many layers. In Sanskrit, the layers are referred to as koshas. Simply put, koshas constitute the whole person. In yoga psychology it is understood that all the layers that form the human being, interlink and ultimately unify as one structure whilst distinction between the layers exist. There are five layers in total, all with their own unique element and structure. They may appear separate but unite together, constituting the whole person.

Annamaya kosha is the physical aspect of the human body. It needs food, water, and air for survival. Pranamaya kosha is the energy needed for existence. It is vital, as it is composed of pranic energy. However, both koshas are necessary to provide a basis for the soul. Manomaya kosha is the mental layer and is responsible for regulating thoughts and action, whereas vijnanamaya kosha is the layer that connects the human body and the mind. It is the accumulation of knowledge and experience that brings wisdom. Anandamaya kosha is the joy, love, and peace that is underneath or inner most to ātman, or the self. To use a metaphor that each layer represents a lamp shade, there would be five in total. The lightbulb itself would best describe ātman. There are many branches of yoga that take complimentary paths to enlightenment, among them bhakti, hatha, jnana, karma, mantra, tantric, kundalini, and raja yoga. Through a series of poses, pranayama, shatkarmas, meditation, and relaxation, the goal ultimately remains the same. We all have a desire for a meaningful life, to have purpose and direction, to find happiness and love. I certainly don't have the answers. However, I can be guided by the knowledge and experience of those before me. In the wisdom of Patanjali's sutras and the expansive text and conversation between Lord Krishna and Arjuna in the Bhagavad Gita, we can receive some insights. With daily practice and devotion, we can raise our vibration and heighten our experience here on earth.

What I have found interesting is what I have learnt about myself through my practice and understanding of yoga. Yoga poses remain the same, but we are constantly changing within them. Likewise in life, we are constantly exposed to similar situations, but how we respond may be different. To have an understanding of what makes up the layers of our existence and the experiences of the past that constitute our personality is of great significance. Furthermore, to know that fate and karma are real but only predetermined to a point, has had a huge impact on my understanding of life. This is what I have learnt from yoga, but it's only the beginning!

GLOSSARY

Ajapa Dharana	meditational practice in which a mantra is repeated
Ajna Chakra	psychic centre in the mid-brain
Amrit	psychic "nectar" secreted in bindu moving down to Vishuddhi chakra
Anahata	unstuck, no restrictions
Anahata Chakra	area related to the heart
Annamaya Kosha	the physical aspect of the body, relating to the level of existence
Asana	a yoga position
Ashram	yogic community where aspirants of yoga live together
Ashwa Sanchalanasana	horse rider's pose
Atman	the pure self, beyond mind and body
Bandha	the contraction of muscles around a joint
Bhatki Yoga	the yoga of devotion
Bindu	a chakra situated at the back of the head

Cerebrospinal Fluid	the fluid that cushions the brain and spinal cord
Chakra	wheel or energy centre, responsible for specific functions
Dhanurasana	bow pose
Ida	the feminine energy, or nadi
Iyengar Yoga	a style of yoga designed by BKS Iyengar
Karma	actions, the inherent subconscious imprints that affect a person's behaviour and personality
Karma Yoga	actions performed for the benefit of a group, not for personal gain
Koshas	layers or sheaths
Lord Shiva	archetypal renunciate and yogi
Manomaya Kosha	dealing with the mind
Mantra	a sound or series of words that is repeated
Moola Bundha	the contraction of muscles at the base of the spine. Used to awaken Mooladhara
Mooladhara	the energy centre that controls the "will to live," our survival instincts
Mudra	position or movement of the body to harness energy in the body.
Nadis	psychic channels for the distribution of prana in the body
Neti	saltwater wash for the nasal cavity
Nirvana	enlightenment, bliss
OM	mantra or sound repeated
Pineal Gland	a small endocrine gland responsible for the production of melatonin
Pingala	the masculine energy or nadi

Prakriti	the underlying influence of energy
Prana	the life force in the body located between the heart and lungs, loosely referred to as the breath
Pranamaya kosha	the layer that refers to the flow of prana in the body
Sahasrara	the crown chakra
Samadhi	bliss, enlightenment
Surya Namaskara	sun salutation pose
Trataka	meditational practice
Uddiyana bandha	abdominal lock
Vairagya	non-attachment
Vedas	yoga texts
Vijnanamaya	wisdom and knowledge
Vishnu	Hindu god, preserver of the universe
Vishuddhi	chakra the chakra located at the throat
Vritti	modifications of the mind arising in the consciousness
Yoga	To unite mind, body and soul
Yoga Nidra	a relaxation practice
Yoga Sutras	text written by Patanjali, offering guidance along the path of yoga

REFERENCES

Chapter 1

www.abc.net.au.

www.asitis.com/12/12.html.

www.hinduwebsite.com/devotion.html.

www.in.geocities.com/gitabykrishna/e-gandhi.html.

www.skys.com.au.

www.yogajournal.com.

www.yogapractice.com.au/sanga.

www.nhmrc.gov.au/files,publications,attachments.

www.simplebackpain.com/anatomyofthebackhtml.

Saraswati, Swami Satyananda. *Four Chapters on Freedom: Commentary on the Yoga Sutras of Patanjali,* India: Yoga Publications Trust, 2000.

Saraswati, Swami Niranjanananda. *Yoga Darshan,* India: Yoga Publications Trust, 2002.

Yoga Sadhana Panorama, India: Yoga Publications Trust, 1997.

Shivashakti. *Stress, The Stress Response and How Stress Affects the Body,* SYTA Seminar at Enmore, May 2004. Newsletter of the Satyananda Yoga Teacher's Association.

Cousins, M. J. *Manage Your Pain,* AU: ABC Books, 2011.

Chapter 2

http://indiaexpress.com/mind/yoga.

http:/www.theosophy.org/tlodocs/yogasutras.

http://www.yogatourism.com/yoga.htm.

Saraswati, Swami Satyananda. *Asana Pranayama Mudra Banda,* Bihar, India: Yoga Publications Trust, 2002.

———. *Kundalini Tantra,* Bihar, India: Yoga Publications Trust, 2001.

Chapter 3

http://indiaexpress.com/mind/yoga.

http://www.yogatourism.com/yoga.htm.

http:/www.theosophy.org/tlodocs/yogasutras.

Saraswati, Swami Satyananda. *Asana Pranayama Mudra Banda,* Bihar, India: Yoga Publications Trust, 2002.

———. *Kundalini Tantra,* Bihar, India: Yoga Publications Trust, 2001.

Chapter 4

www.goodreads.com/quotes113417.

http://www.yogatourism.com/yoga.htm.

www.tantra-kundalini.com/anahata.htm.

Saraswati, Swami Satyananda. *Kundalini Tantra,* Yoga Publications Trust, Bihar, India, 2001

Mandela, N. *Long Walk to Freedom: The Autobiography of Nelson Mandela,* South Africa: Little, Brown and Company, 1994.

Chapter 5

www.william-shakespear.info/shakespear-play-as-you-like-it-html.

www.adishakti.org/subtle_system/vishuddhi_chakra.html.

Satyananda, Swami. *Four Chapters on Freedom: Commentary on the Yoga Sutras of Patanjali,* India: Yoga Publication Trust 2002.

Chapter 6

www.chakras.net/energy-centers/vishuddhi.

Swami Satyananda Saraswati. *Kundalini Tantra,* Bihar, India: Yoga Publications Trust, 2001.

Niranjan, Swami. *Yoga Sadhana Panorama,* India: Yoga Publications Trust 1997, 161.

_____. *Yoga Sadhana Panorama,* India: Yoga Publication Trust 1997, 263.

_____. *Yoga Darshan,* India: Yoga Publications Trust, 2002, 111.

_____. *Yoga Darshan,* India: Yoga Publications Trust, 2002, 114.

_____. *Yoga Darshan,* India: Yoga Publication Trust, 2002, 136.

_____. *Yoga Sadhana Panorama,* India: Yoga Publications Trust, 1997.

Satyananda, Swami. *Four Chapters on Freedom: Commentary on the Yoga Sutras of Patanjali,* India: Yoga Publications Trust, 2000, 36.

Chapter 7

Sivananda, Swami. *Bhagavad Gita,* India: Forest Academy Press, 2003, 300–05.

www.goodreads.com/quote553646.

www.asitis.com.

www.asitis.com/12/12,html.

www.asitis.com/12/12,html.

www.yogapractice.com.au/sanga.

www.bhagavadgitaasitis.com.

www.hinduwebsite.com/devotion.htm.

www.yogajournal.com/wisdom/462.

www.swamij.com/yoga-sutras.htm.

www.theosophy.org/tlodocs/yogasutras.